THE

INSIDER'S GUIDE TO FINDING THE
RIGHT JOB

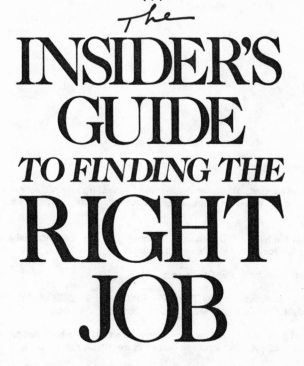

The
INSIDER'S GUIDE
TO FINDING THE
RIGHT JOB

DIANE LEWIS
with
JOE CARROLL

Thomas Nelson Publishers
Nashville

Published in Nashville, Tennessee, by Thomas Nelson, Inc. and distributed in Canada by Lawson Falle, Ltd., Cambridge, Ontario.

Printed in the United States of America.

Scripture quotations are from THE NEW KING JAMES VERSION of the Bible. Copyright © 1979, 1980, 1982, Thomas Nelson, Inc., Publishers.

To avoid grammatical problems, the pronouns *he* and *his* have been used predominantly and do not reflect sexism on the part of the publisher or author.

ISBN 0-8407-3107-8

1 2 3 4 5 6 — 91 90 89 88 87

To
Reverend Jerry K. Rose,
Dr. Douglas Stevans,

and

Pastor Ron Hembree

More than any others,
you are responsible
for my growth as a Christian.

*Special thanks and blessings to my friend
and partner, Carol A. Ritzke, who
provided tolerance as well as advice;
George Puia;
Joyce Gallager;
my children, Dwight and Bill,
for not having as much of their mother
as they are used to;
William J. Walker, my brother,
for telling me I can do anything.*

———— ◇◇◇ ————

CONTENTS

INTRODUCTION

This is a book of simple steps and a book of secrets.

The steps are simple because the task before you is simple. That's the first thing you have to understand and believe: getting a job is *easy*.

The idea that getting a job is easy might be difficult to accept if you've been out of work for some time—if you're leaving the familiar, comforting world of school and facing the unknown job market for the very first time—if you're returning to the job market after a prolonged absence to raise your family—or if you're considering the challenge of a job with more responsibility than the one you have now.

In other words, this book is addressed to anybody who is about to offer himself or herself to the working world.

Offering yourself as a job candidate implies that people will be making judgments about you. That's a disturbing prospect. So let's face it at the outset: looking for a job scares you. You're not alone though. It scares everybody.

To help you understand and accept the simple steps to job-hunting success, I'll share some secrets, too: the "insider information" of the personnel recruiting industry. You'll learn what we interviewers look for in job applicants and what makes us choose one applicant over another.

The foundations for all that you'll read are faith and experience. As to faith, I believe in a God who loves us and wants what's best for us. I'm also convinced that those who live by faith in Him are better prepared than anyone else for job hunting as well as every other activity of life. As to experience, I've been in the recruiting business most of my working life. During my more than twenty years in the personnel field, I've talked with tens of thousands of job seekers. During the last twenty years, as president of my own company, I've talked with almost as many employers. Everything in this book has evolved from my practical experience and from my personal faith in the Lord, whom I met for the first time a few years ago.

Let me warn you about a problem you might have with the truths you'll read here. You might be reluctant to agree that any procedures so simple can be so effective. But that's the whole point. If the simple steps in this book were intended to deal with a complex problem, they wouldn't work. But the problem is simple; getting a job is *easy*. Companies want and *need* to hire you. You don't need any tricks to convince them. You just need to avoid giving them reasons *not* to hire you.

Because of all you've heard and read, however, and perhaps because of your personal bad experience of job hunting, you may feel differently. Do you dread looking for a job? Do you think that finding work is tough? Are you convinced that you'll feel rejected? Do you fret over what you need to write, what you need to wear, what you need to say?

It's understandable if you feel that way. But you'll have ample evidence before we're through that those feelings are wrong. You'll prove to yourself that getting a job is the kind of straightforward task you can handle easily. You'll see that the simplest job-hunting techniques can be the best job-hunting techniques. You'll come to believe that getting a job is in fact easy.

I know the simple job-hunting procedures and techniques you'll be learning are appropriate because I've seen them work time and again. Their effectiveness has been reaffirmed with dazzling success at the job seminars I've conducted for the past couple of years in partnership with WCFC-TV/38, our fine Christian station in Chicago. This book contains much of the material discussed at the seminars and compensates for our inability to conduct them in every city where they're needed. Let me give you just one example of their effectiveness.

A few weeks after a recent job seminar, I was asked by a philanthropic organization to conduct a search to fill a new position. The leaders of the organization awarded the contract to my company because they knew of our job seminars and assumed, reasonably enough, that our attendees would be outstanding choices for their particular needs.

There had been more than 750 attendees at that seminar (I'm sorry now that we didn't keep a precise count). When my associate and I began to telephone those attendees to invite them to interview, we got quite a surprise. One after another, the people we contacted thanked us for calling but said they had already found jobs. In fact, it seemed that we were getting this message with far greater frequency than our experience would have led us to expect.

You can imagine how curious we became. We had a prime job to offer, and our labor pool was drying up before our eyes. So we continued to call attendees in our spare moments and in the evenings and on weekends over a four-week period. By the time we finished, we had long since filled the job, but we continued our calls because we were too curious to stop.

We were able to contact 608 attendees, of whom 502 were *already employed*.

I want to stipulate that there was nothing scientific about this survey. Neither of us had the training to analyze the results statistically. But my experience tells me that one should not expect over 80 percent of the people from such a seminar to be employed less than two months later. Common sense probably suggests the same interpretation to you.

We'll often rely in this book on the evidence of common sense and secular experience, as we just did in that example. But I wouldn't want that to give you the idea that you can achieve success all on your own, by your own intellect and through your own effort. In job hunting, as in every other area of life, God directs. And while the basic strategy and techniques of job hunting in this book are effective for anyone, I'm convinced that sincere Christian faith is a definite asset in the process, as I'll explain in Chapter 1.

I also insist that you must become involved with the book. There will be some exercises for you to do, sort of "aerobics for the soul." Please don't limit yourself by just reading the book, nodding your head in agreement, and then setting it aside. Cooperate with the approach. Do the exercises.

Now here's our plan: first, let me remind you of one of the secrets—the most important one—the secret of what employment interviewers look for—the secret that determines who gets a job and who keeps looking for one—the secret that's so important that we'll come back to it repeatedly. "The Secret to Getting Hired" is the subject of the first part of the book. I know you might be tempted to skip ahead to the second part, "How to Do It: An Insider's Techniques," but I urge you to resist temptation. "The Secret to Getting Hired" is indispensable to your success as a job hunter. It will empty your mind of all the false and poisonous impressions the world has given you about the simple task of job hunting. We have to empty your mind of this nonsense in order to make room for the final goal: filling you up again with faith and truth and hope.

Not to mention the joy and excitement of your brand-new job.

PART I
THE SECRET TO GETTING HIRED

CHAPTER 1

The One Thing Employers Want Most

= ◇ =

Here's what typically happens when I interview candidates for a job I'm being paid to fill. Frequently, more than one qualified applicant responds to a newspaper ad. In such cases, it's the practice in our industry to present all the qualified candidates to the employer for the final decision. This gives me the opportunity to play a little mental game in which I try to guess which one of the candidates will be offered the job.

I always win this little game, because even though the candidates may be roughly equal in terms of their skills, education, and experience, the job *always* goes to that candidate who knows the secret to getting hired. The job *always* goes to that candidate who displays enthusiasm, confidence, determination, sincerity, and cheerfulness.

The job always goes to that candidate, in other words, who displays what I would call a "Christian attitude." That attitude is the secret to getting hired.

I call this a Christian attitude because it grows most naturally out of a recognition that the Lord wants His people to be productive and happy. The outward signs of this recognition are the attributes mentioned above: enthusiasm, confidence, determination, sincerity, and cheerfulness. But *anyone* who genuinely displays such an attitude will have little trouble getting hired.

> ● **Rule 1 is that when there's more than one qualified candidate for a job (which is most of the time), the job *always* goes to the candidate with the best (that is, Christian) attitude, whether that candidate is a Christian or not.**

Every employer in the world wants to surround himself with employees who are cheerful and enthusiastic. If you've ever been in a supervisory position or been charged with the responsibility of hiring a new employee, you know how true that is. Enthusiastic employees are productive employees. As the business writer Maxwell Maltz noted, "A human being always acts and feels and performs in accordance with what he imagines to be true about himself and his environment." If your attitude causes you to perceive yourself to be a winner, your work will reflect that perception, and employers know it. I have seen employers reject a more experienced candidate in favor of a candidate of slightly lesser qualification, solely on the basis of an enthusiastic, winning attitude displayed by the successful candidate.

Now here's the thing that puzzles me. Who should have a better attitude than a Christian? Christians have been promised in John 10:10, "I have come that they may have life, and that they may have it more abundantly." What more do we need to make us cheerful? The Lord told us in Luke 17:21 that "the kingdom of God is within you"; what other knowledge do we need to make us confident and unafraid?

There's an excitement, a thrill, a tingle, that a Christian feels when he embraces the Lord at the moment of rebirth.

That excitement ought to spill over abundantly into his secular life. We should not put the light of our Christian faith, as the Lord said in Matthew 5:15, "under a basket," but should display it prominently for all to see. Our joy at our salvation as Christians should be evident in our gleaming attitudes.

That's why it's hard for me to understand how a Christian can be unemployed on any but the most temporary of bases. I know from experience that a good attitude gets hired before good skills. And I know that Christians have the best, most vigorous attitudes in the world—or should have anyway. It seems that employers should be lining up to hire Christians.

Why, then, don't we put on our earnest, sincere smiles when we interview for jobs? Why don't we show that confident, energetic attitude all the time? I can only conclude that too many of us Christians put our faith and joy away for Sundays. Take those Christian emotions out and show them to the world and, most especially, to anyone who interviews you for a job!

> ● **Rule 2 is not to be bashful about letting the world see the positive, joyous attitude that comes from your faith in the Lord and from His love for you. Your enthusiasm, confidence, determination, sincerity, and cheerfulness are in demand. And the most apparent of these five to a personnel interviewer is enthusiasm.**

BARBARA'S STORY

A few years ago, one of my clients asked me to find an experienced secretary to work in his busy office. The job specifications stipulated good communication ability, professional appearance, and topnotch secretarial skills. The "specs" went on at some length, in fact, defining in precise detail the typing speed, degree of typing accuracy, and level of shorthand that would be acceptable. All in all, the specs made a very precise, businesslike document that gave no hint that attitude was the principal criterion for this job.

It's my business to know the "secret," however, the secret that people make hiring decisions based first and foremost on the attitude of the candidate. Skills, talents, appearance, and all the rest are important, of course. But enthusiasm weighs more heavily than any other single factor. As Karl Menninger, a founder of the famed Menninger Clinic, put it, "Attitude is more important than fact."

For this assignment, I found several well-qualified professional secretaries, all with the skills set forth in the specs. I also met one young woman who was fresh from high school, where she'd taken a few secretarial courses. Because of her relative inexperience, she was a little below the required skill levels in every category but one: the shorthand category. She was more than "a little below" the acceptable level in that category—she didn't have any shorthand at all.

What she did have, though, was a strikingly refreshing attitude. She had taken the trouble to read about the company at the public library, and she liked what she learned. She was enthusiastic about working there and didn't view the position as "just a job," which described the orientation of some of the other candidates. She didn't say she wanted *a* job, *any* job; she said she seriously wanted *that* job, that *particular* job. She was prepared to come in early and stay late when the need was there. She didn't ask about the vacation policy or how long the lunch period was. She really gave the impression that she was ready, willing, and able to get to work. She was all fired up, she let it show, and she didn't care who knew it.

Because I know what employers really want, I decided my client would have to meet this dynamo.

I eventually introduced four candidates to my client, one of whom was Barbara, the young woman I've just told you about. He interviewed each one at length and carefully reviewed their scores on the skills tests I'd given them. When I went into his office later to learn which candidate would receive the offer, he thanked me for the high-caliber talent I'd shown him. He admitted that he'd intentionally set his requirements at an extremely high level, higher than was absolutely necessary, on the theory that this would produce our most experienced, most skilled candidates.

I told him I would pass his kind remarks along to all the candidates involved. I was sure they'd appreciate his recognition of their mastery of the secretarial profession. Then I asked him which of the outstanding candidates he'd chosen.

He paused a bit before answering. The expression on his face told me he was more than a little surprised at the judgment he'd made. "Let's go with Barbara," he said.

Of course. I wasn't surprised in the least. It's the choice Rule 1 would have predicted: the job *always* goes to the candidate with the best attitude.

This man had been a client of mine for some time. We knew each other well, and we trusted each other. So I thought it would be okay if I had a little fun with him. I said, "But Barbara didn't score as well on the tests as the other candidates."

"Well, she didn't do too badly," he said.

"But she was below the minimums you said you'd consider."

"Yeah, but she was pretty close."

"And she doesn't take shorthand at all. Not even a little bit."

"I think I'll buy one of those dictating gizmos—you know,

those tape recorder things. Then she can type from it directly. It's probably more efficient to do dictation that way, anyhow."

I tried to look confused. "But why did you choose her over those better qualified?"

"There's something about her," he said. "I think she really wants the company to do well. She's sincere, you know? She has an air of—excitement, I guess I'd have to say. She seems full of energy." He thought for a moment. Then he said, "I want people like that around me. People like her keep me ahead in the business world."

> ● Rule 3 is that you can't trick a good in-
> terviewer. Your attitude has to be real. A
> phony attitude is as transparent as clean
> glass.

The case I've just told you about is not unusual. In fact, it's common to see an employer "reach" for a candidate with a good attitude. So let me tell you why I remember this particular incident so well. The company that hired Barbara eventually relocated the plant down South. Because Barbara didn't want to uproot her family, she decided to stay in the Chicago area. So she came onto the job market again, just as enthusiastic and energetic as before. Even though I'm in the personnel business, I can't resist that glowing enthusiasm any more than any other employer; Barbara eventually came to work for me!

Of course, you know why she got the job—attitude. She's not a secretary at my company; she's one of our most successful consultants now. And the reason? Well, I guess you know what I'd say, don't you?

= ◇ =

If you're afraid of the prospect of presenting yourself to the job market, it's because the positive, confident attitude God wants you to have has been suppressed. It's been suppressed by the overpowering importance of work in our society. Certainly, work means income. If you've lost your job, if you've recently become a single parent, or if you're just starting to make your way in the world for the first time, you're intensely aware of the sweetness of the regular income that a job provides.

But work means even more than income, doesn't it? Work has something to do with your self-esteem, your self-respect. Before we begin recovering that golden attitude of yours, it might be helpful to examine why not having a job is such a crushing defeat for us, why work means something to us all that is beyond our need for income.

CHAPTER 2

Why Work Makes You Happy

= ◇ =

Before I went into the personnel field, I suppose I would
have felt (if I thought about it at all) that someone who lost his
job through his own fault would feel worse about it than somebody who was unemployed for reasons beyond his control.
That is, it would have seemed logical to me that a worker who
lost his job for, say, poor performance or absence would have
been more ashamed and more depressed than someone who
was displaced by new technology. And both would have been
sadder than the returning worker or the new worker who was
too young to have had any meaningful employment yet.

I don't remember exactly when it was, but I gradually came
to understand that such an assumption, however logical, was
wrong, that the *reason* why someone has no job is less important to his emotional health than the simple *fact* that he has no
job. It's the condition of unemployment that is devastating in
itself. Regardless of whose "fault" it is, regardless of age,
race, sex, or circumstances, being unemployed is truly a
lonely and bitter experience.

The case of a man I interviewed recently is a good example.
Frank had worked for over twenty years at a financial institution that had suddenly and unexpectedly come to well-
publicized hard times. Management felt compelled to
terminate many of the employees, among whom was this hap-
less man.

The shock to those let go was enormous; until shortly before the bad news was made public, the employees had been told that their company was doing extremely well. The company also had a long history of paternalism. These two factors justified the general feeling that anyone who worked there had a job for life, as long as he performed up to expectations. And Frank was a solid, loyal employee with a fine record on the job. He identified with the corporation strongly and deeply, almost as though it were a member of his own family.

And then they "let him go." Not because he'd done anything wrong, but "to save costs."

Nonetheless, Frank wasn't angry or vengeful when I met him; he seemed only to be deeply ashamed. I thought his reaction was inappropriate because he'd had nothing to do with the company's downfall. Yet he choked up frequently during our interview. Tears of shame and grief puddled in his eyes as he reviewed the twenty-some years he had invested in the company. They showed that he'd experienced a trauma similar to the death of a loved one.

Even though I'm a professional who should remain aloof and objective, I was overcome by immense pity at the woeful sight he presented. The image came to me of wretched Job, sitting disconsolately in the ashes, beset by disaster not of his own making.

Clearly, unemployment left Frank demoralized. But why was the impact so great? Remember that he had no part in the company's decline; there was no reason for him to feel guilt or shame. But he did, just as surely as if the whole mess had been his fault.

He couldn't have been feeling financially insecure, either. He'd had a professional position and had earned a good income. He admitted that he had some money put away and that he was in no immediate danger of financial collapse.

Nor could he have been worried that his prospects for future employment were anything less than bright. He was well educated and highly skilled, and his talents and record were exemplary. I knew he would land on his feet, and I think he knew it, too.

Why, then, his depression—almost to the point of despair? I was certain he'd find a wonderful job soon, and I couldn't understand his despondency. I asked him if he would try to explain it.

He said that he had always taken his job very seriously and that it meant a great deal to him.

"Yes," I said, "that much I can see. But I still don't see why you're so down. After all, with the talents God has given you, you'll find another fine job easily, probably even better than the one you had. And it won't take long, either."

"I know you're right," he snuffled. "But in the meantime, I'm cut off."

"'Cut off'? What does that mean?"

"I guess it means that I'm not who I used to be anymore. I used to belong."

I still wasn't sure I was following him. He saw my confusion and tried again.

"I used to have purpose. I used to have a function," he said. "I used to have a place to go every day where everybody knew me and liked me and respected me. You know what I mean?"

I nodded. I was beginning to understand something about being unemployed.

"Now, I'm not the same person I used to be," he continued. "That's why I feel so bad. I don't know who I am anymore. I just feel like I'm nobody."

Frank's case exposes one of the biggest lies about work (it's also a terribly unkind remark): "People don't want to work; they'd rather be on welfare." Nothing could be further from the truth. Aren't we all like Frank, needing and loving our work? In all my years in the personnel profession, I have never—*never*—met a person who didn't want to work and to work conscientiously and vigorously, if given the opportunity.

But Frank's case also tells us something about the relationship between work and self-identity. A great part of who one *is,* is tied up with what one *does.* In other words, society often assumes a direct relation between your work and your worth as a person. Maybe it shouldn't be that way. But our task is to work with how a situation *is,* not with how it *should* be. And your work is a big part of your identity, not only to your image of yourself but to everybody else's image of you, too.

Consider what happens when you meet someone socially for the first time. After you exchange names, the next question is likely to be, "What do you do for a living?" or "Where do you work?" Not having an acceptable answer to this fundamental question is disastrous to your self-image.

Some people might argue that this view of your work as a fundamental part of yourself is a purely social artifact; that is, an invention of our modern, success-oriented society. But the association of your self-esteem with your work is so persistent that it is probably basic to human nature. In the Middle Ages, for example, when most modern Anglo-Saxon surnames came into being, a person often used the name of his profession to identify himself; hence, Phil "Farmer," George "Smith," James "Cooper."

Incidentally, I've never yet met anybody named Harry "Hopeless" or Wally "Worthless." Everybody, you see, has a value in God's eyes, a value that is inestimable, a value such that, in the justly famous words of John 3:16, God "gave His only begotten Son, that whoever believes in Him should not perish but have everlasting life."

The Lord has ensured that you needn't be a loser. His sacrifice turned sinners into winners—winners like you.

● **Rule 4 is that you have value and worth, imbued in you by God and validated by Christ's sacrifice.**

This rule is an important one to keep in mind. Discussing unemployment and recognizing the misery that comes with not having a job to call your own are necessary if you're going to get rid of that misery. At the same time, though, it's painful to look at such emotions honestly and closely. So this is a good time for us to recognize your worth and to recall that the Lord recognizes it, too. It's a good time to remind you of how important you really are.

It's been my experience that people tend to grossly underestimate their own worth, particularly when they feel the sting of unemployment. If there were a way to measure your own worth as a person, I would advise you to add at least 10 percent to your assessment. It's curious that we don't rate ourselves as generously as the Lord rates us. Make a conscious effort to see the importance He places on you as we continue to look at the negative emotions that surround unemployment and job seeking.

I thought the advice of a specialist might be helpful when writing about those emotions. A friend of mine is an industrial trainer and an expert on motivational theory. He's also a colleague; we've worked together closely on more than one project. I asked him to discuss with me the emotional aspects of being out of work. When I explained that I planned to write this book, he was shocked.

"How can you write a Christian book about working?" he

asked. "I admit it's an important subject, and the results of your job seminars have been nothing short of miraculous. But the subject seems so—well, so *secular.*"

As a Christian, I've always relied faithfully on the authority of Scripture. I reminded him that Jesus chose working men for His disciples and that many of His parables took work experiences for their themes. I even surprised him by speculating that Jesus Himself might have had personal knowledge of blisters from the good, strenuous work in Joseph's shop.

"Still," he responded, "work seems to be a concern of this world. I'm not at all convinced that it's a worthy subject for Christian dialogue."

My friend is a deeply devout man. Maybe that's why he didn't think of issues such as work and unemployment as being associated with religion or the attitude that religion instills in us believers. As the book progressed and as I spoke with experts in fields other than my own, I found that this interpretation is not at all uncommon.

Many people look upon work as a strictly secular concern, a worldly activity beneath the Lord's interest. Some even view work as a scourge, as unpleasant drudgery, far removed from heavenly concerns. To be sure, part of God's curse for mankind in Genesis 3:19, "In the sweat of your face you shall eat bread," might be thought to justify such feelings.

But ignoring the importance and meaning of work is contrary to God's intentions for us after the Fall. It's also at odds with human nature. Our society has understood for hundreds of years this relevance of work to God's plans and to the human ego.

People have long realized the value of honest work well done. Not only does productive work have obvious positive results in goods made or services performed, but it also helps to discipline sinful human nature. This understanding led to an admiration of honest, steady work as an outstanding example of self-discipline. The determination to "do the world's work" has even come to be described as the "Protestant work ethic."

The need to do work in the world is not irrelevant to God's plan; indeed, work is an integral part of God's plan for you. Labor is a calling, not a commodity. Work is a divine commandment, and even Christian slaves were admonished to carry out their tasks willingly, recognizing the divine nature of work: "Servants, obey in all things your masters according to the flesh, not with eye-service, as men-pleasers, but in sincerity of heart, fearing God" (Col. 3:22).

Paul was saying something about enthusiasm for work, wasn't he? He was saying that it is not enough for us to simply work in a mediocre, dispassionate, uncaring manner. In the next verse, he further encouraged, "And whatever you do, do it heartily, as to the Lord and not to men."

The divine plan for you, therefore, requires that you work wholeheartedly, as in Ecclesiastes 9:10: "Whatever your hand finds to do, do it with your might."

The rewards of earthly work are put into perspective in 1 Thessalonians 4:11–12, "Work with your own hands, as we commanded you, that you may walk properly toward those who are outside, and that you may lack nothing." The *real* wages of honest work, therefore, are respect and independence: the respect of others and your financial independence from them. These are generous wages indeed.

Small wonder, then, that one who is out of work and deprived of the privilege of walking properly and with dignity, deprived of the gift from God that honest work can be, feels the sting of despair.

THE CYCLE OF JOBLESSNESS

The cycle of joblessness, then, is this: awareness of having no job brings immediate distress. Only the fact of your joblessness is important from the standpoint of your emotions, not the reason for it. You, like every person who's not gainfully employed, feel shame and grief, regardless of whether those feelings are justified by the facts. The thought of looking for a job means facing up to the judgments you feel will be made about you, which adds fear to the list of your emotional baggage.

Because you think you have a "worldly" problem, you decide to "row your own boat" instead of asking the Lord to take the oars. But your depression makes you easy prey for the myths that surround unemployment, the half-truths and outright fallacies that make you conclude it's hard to get a job. These false ideas make your plight seem even worse, and you begin to wallow in self-pity and hopelessness. Your misery smothers that ebullient attitude Christians should have.

When you let your good attitude take a back seat, a prospective employer chooses another candidate over you, somebody who's more "up." You're disappointed, and your self-esteem slips still another notch. You'll probably be even more of a sad sack on the next job interview, with perfectly predictable results.

And down and down you go.

Sound familiar?

The way to break the downward spiral of despair that results from joblessness is through faith, the kind of faith in the Lord and in yourself that will shine through and produce the warm glow of a Christian attitude. And that attitude is irresistible to employers.

But to make room for that faith, we have to clear away some of those diabolical myths that blind the eyes of the job seeker just as effectively as the scales that covered the eyes of Saul. That's what happens in the next chapter.

CHAPTER 3

Popular Myths about the Job Market

= ◇ =

As with all important aspects of life, everybody assumes he knows everything there is to know about the world of work. This apparent obviousness prevents most people from thinking deeply about working and about the process of looking for work. Misinterpretations are, of course, commonplace and are spread around among otherwise well-meaning people until a mythology is built up that injures your job-seeking ability. It's a mythology that poisons your mind, making you believe some things about job hunting that have the sound of truth but not the substance.

Some job-hunting fallacies are common to us all. Some are unique to you alone and are the negative images you create about yourself in your mind. You'll be pleased to know that both kinds are easy to dispel because you can't be defeated by your emotions unless you allow it.

Later we'll look at some of the wrong ideas individuals develop about themselves, but in this chapter we'll examine those myths that *all* of us believe. And believe them we do. We believe them so thoroughly, in fact, that we don't even trouble ourselves to question their validity anymore.

We've already looked at one of those myths in the last chapter: the one that says you don't really want to work because work is unpleasant, the one that says you're content to collect unemployment rather than eager to collect your job. We saw that nonsense for what it was by discovering the basic goodness of work.

NOT ENOUGH JOBS

Another myth about the job market is that there aren't enough good jobs to go around. Here's how a fallacy like that gets started. From time to time, every free economy can lose some of the powerhouse character that is its traditional hallmark. In fact, that's to be expected: slowdowns are a part of the free-market cycle.

But whenever the economy slows down, the news media drum the bad news into our heads with great vigor. This happened, you'll remember, in the late seventies and early eighties. It seemed as if lead stories stressing the scarcity of jobs would become a permanent feature of the nightly national news. Banner headlines in newspapers told us that there just weren't any jobs to be had—period. In fact, we formed the impression that anyone who was blessed to have a job was in danger of losing it because times were so grim.

Will Rogers made famous the remark that "I only know what I read in the papers." Had he been around to read the papers during the last recession, he would have thought he was the only person in the country who was working. The news media scared us all very badly, both the employed and the unemployed alike. Remember?

Well, it wasn't true then, at least not to the extent we were led to believe, and it certainly isn't true now.

The fact is that jobs are *plentiful*.

The reason the news media misled us is simple: good news doesn't sell newspapers. The problem is that all this bad news is repeated every day during even the most minor of recessions. This incessant repetition not only saps the vitality and enthusiasm of the job seeker, but it also gives him a perfect excuse to avoid looking for a job.

> ● **Rule 5 is that jobs are the most plentiful fruits of God's blessing on our mighty free economy. As I always tell people at our job seminars, "In God's economy there is no unemployment."**

You couldn't be expected to believe this statement without proof. You've been told so often and so loudly that jobs are hard to come by that you ought to demand some evidence before you accept my statements to the contrary. My friend Chuck Cannon recognized this need when he spoke at one of our recent job seminars. Chuck is a public relations expert and, as you might expect, has close ties to the Chicago newspapers. He exercised his contacts there to determine the demand for workers in Chicago.

He estimated that the *Chicago Tribune* runs more than 1,200,000 employment want ads annually, and the Chicago *Sun-Times* runs about another 800,000. That's *2 million* want ads in just our two principal newspapers. Add to this the want ads in our many suburban papers (of which there were too many for Chuck to research directly), the *Wall Street Journal,* and the various trade magazines, and you have some idea of the immensity of the job market today.

Of course, I use Chicago for many of my examples because both my business and my ministry are located here and it's the market I know best. The market in your area may well be different. But relative to the population of your area, there's no reason to suspect that your job opportunities are any less overwhelming.

Furthermore, the want ad figures don't tell the whole story. As I look out my office window, I can see a business down the street, one of the overnight mail companies. The Help Wanted sign in the window is actually bigger than the sign stating the name of the company; the firm appears to want new employees rather badly, wouldn't you say?

Recently, I drove out to the Clearing Industrial District to pay a call on a client. Clearing is an industrial park on the South Side of Chicago. It may be a little bigger and a little older but is in no other way different from any other industrial park across the nation.

Joe owns a manufacturing company in Clearing. His factory produces dinette tables and chairs for shipment all over the world. I was there to discuss a bookkeeping position that had recently been created due to the company's continuing expansion.

"Well, Joe," I said, "business must be good if you need another bookkeeper."

"Diane, we've really been blessed," he answered. "We've worked very hard to make our product line the best in the business, and it's paying off. The only thing that keeps us from doing even more business is our inability to produce more output. You see, I just can't get enough workers."

Joe has a policy of paying one of the highest hourly wages in the area. His high pay scale should have ensured lines of willing workers outside the plant. I suppose I looked surprised at his remark.

"It's true," he said. "I've needed an operator for our new numerically controlled punch press for almost a month now, and there are no takers."

"Maybe there aren't many people who know how to operate one of those—what did you call it?"

"An N/C punch press. You're right, of course. It's a highly

skilled job. But I'd be willing to train somebody. Say, could you recruit somebody for that kind of job?"

My company had handled his executive and office personnel needs, which are our specialties, for many years. I had to admit we didn't have the expertise to recruit production workers. But it sounded like a challenging, rewarding opportunity. I wondered out loud why he hadn't been able to hire somebody. "How have you been advertising the position?" I asked.

He took me to the window and pointed to a big Help Wanted display sign out front. I had to admit I'd walked right past it without seeing it.

Then I looked down the main street of the industrial park. From his third-floor window, I could see plenty of signs like Joe's, announcing jobs for painters, assemblers, dock workers, and on and on. Don't let anyone tell you the "smokestack" industries are dead. They're a lot smaller than they used to be, and they've dispersed to industrial parks. They're more technology intensive and less labor intensive nowadays. They may be big *users* of steel, coal, and other resources rather than big *producers*. But they're out there, and they're hiring.

How many jobless people have gone right past those signs and never noticed them, just as I did? How many of us limit ourselves by continuing to think of ourselves as steelworkers or autoworkers or mineworkers when we should think of ourselves simply as workers? How many opportunities does such a mind-set cause us to ignore or not even to notice? Maybe we all need to pray not only for more jobs in our economy, but also for the sensitivity to recognize the jobs that are all around us.

I really mean that: jobs are all around us no matter where we find ourselves. They can be found even in those "depressed" areas that one of our myths says you have to leave if you want to work. Even in West Virginia, a seriously distressed part of our country where I recently conducted a job seminar, people found work. It wasn't always the work they wanted. Sometimes they had to take a "reality pill" to understand that the jobs they wanted no longer existed. Sometimes they had to swallow hard and start over again, at the bottom.

But even in this economically distressed part of our country, even in a place where there is no Help Wanted section in the newspaper, people found work after a seminar—not so many and not so fast as in a big, diverse city like Chicago, but enough that our sponsor there has asked for another seminar next year.

So when you hear that the only way to find work is to move away, you're hearing another myth. There is *always* opportunity available *everywhere*. You have to learn to recognize it and to accept that fact, even though it may require you to change your outlook. If you want to relocate, do it for the right reasons: because you want to live in the Sun Belt; because you want to be close to other family members who have moved away; because somebody has offered you a *better* job than the one you have; because you want to become a pineapple farmer and that's tough to do in Minnesota.

The point is, there are all sorts of valid reasons for *moving* away, but there are none for *running* away. Believing that life is easier somewhere else tends to work out poorly, as things done for the wrong motives usually do. Looking for work out of town is disruptive to your family life, and it's expensive. I generally recommend that you avoid it unless you have some specific and logical reason or unless, of course, you already have a job lined up at the other end.

There's so much opportunity right at home to be exploited. Think about all the jobs that never get advertised—jobs that only personnel firms know about. In fact, it's an accepted premise in my business that the very best jobs are often the ones that don't get advertised. By way of example, here's just one search assignment being carried out by my firm at the time of this writing. We're staffing a new division of approximately eighty persons for a national company. We're recruiting staff from entry-level clerical positions through the vice president who will manage the division. We're "sourcing" the applicants (which means we're contacting people already in our data base) and have not found it necessary to advertise any of these jobs.

Just think—over eighty prime jobs that don't even show up in the statistics, eighty jobs in the so-called hidden job market. And how many other personnel firms have similar search assignments? I can't tell you because personnel companies don't share that kind of competitive information. But surely, the number must be huge; companies like mine couldn't even exist, much less prosper, unless other companies were willing to pay us big fees to find employees to fill their jobs.

Think about that for a moment. Companies pay us big fees *to find people to fill their jobs*.

And think about all the jobs even personnel companies don't know about—jobs that are made known only to current employees so they can bring in their friends. And you know what? Those companies often pay a "bounty" to their employees for bringing in those friends and helping them to get the jobs!

Not enough jobs to go around? Nonsense! They're so abundant that companies have to pay to find people to fill them. Jobs are all over the place!

> ● **Rule 6 is that there are more jobs looking for people than there are people looking for jobs.**

Here's a challenge to you. Let's begin to examine why you don't have a job. A good way to start is for you to ask yourself the question directly. Why don't you have a job? And if you're blessed with a job currently but feel the need for a better one, why haven't you gotten it?

If your first impulse is to tell me something about unemployment statistics, go back and reread the preceding paragraphs. Most of the things you hear about unemployment and about the difficulty of getting a job are the grossest exaggerations, one part truth and nine parts nonsense. They cunningly make you complacent about being out of work; they make you take your eye off the Lord and blame the economy for your sorry predicament. But there must be other reasons why you're out of work because the one about the scarcity of jobs is just a plain lie.

There are so many jobs that the toughest task facing some young people is choosing a career, so much so that I've recently begun recommending to them the excellent book *Finding a Job You Can Love,* by Ralph Mattson and Arthur Miller (Thomas Nelson, 1982). Being able to pick and choose your job to accommodate your likes and dislikes as that book teaches you to do is a great blessing. It's a freedom that makes us want to shout "Only in America!" and that exposes the notion that there aren't enough jobs for all of us as a myth.

INSUFFICIENT JOB SKILLS

It's a funny thing about these myths concerning work: no sooner is your mind cleansed of one fallacy and you understand how many companies want to hire you—*need* to hire you—than another myth pops up to distract you. The next one has to do with what are commonly referred to as "job skills." The "job skills" fallacy concedes that jobs are available but persuades you that you lack the training necessary to do any of those jobs.

Don't feel too bad if you've ever fallen for this one. Even the president was misled by this widespread popular myth. A few years ago, Ronald Reagan was on TV one night trying to dispel the false idea that jobs were hard to come by. He held up one of the Washington newspapers and commented on the number of want ads that went unfilled week after week. Then he, too, concluded that people lack the skills demanded by all those employers.

Here's the danger of believing that misinterpretation: you'll think that if you don't already have all the skills those jobs require, you don't have a chance of getting hired. And if you don't have a chance of getting hired, there's no point in even trying, right?

The truth is that many employers will provide training on the job to help a new employee gain the skills he needs to perform well, as my client Joe was willing to do. This is most often the case with larger corporations.

For example, a large Chicago company for which my firm has done considerable work has a training department. Among the many training classes offered is the course "Typing and Transcription," which is held on the company's premises for two hours each day, five days a week, for two months. Employees enrolled in the class have the approval of supervisors to spend this time away from the job and in the classroom. The purpose of the course is to help employees upgrade themselves by developing the skill of typing from audiotapes. Typists, especially those who can type quickly and accurately from such tapes, are in short supply in Chicago. This particular company pays a "machine skills premium" over and above normal salary to employees who have mastered this skill and others like it. Over the years, dozens of this corporation's employees have considerably improved their career satisfaction (to say nothing of their incomes) by taking advantage of such training.

That explains why employers hire a good attitude before they hire good skills. They can give you the skills through training, but you determine your attitude.

Notice, however, that this training is available only to employees of the company. This means that the first step is to get hired by such a company in the first place. It's like the old recipe for rabbit stew that begins, "First catch a rabbit. . . ."

And understand that having gotten a job at such a company through the appeal of your enthusiastic attitude isn't enough to guarantee continuing success. The training opportunities at this company are offered only to employees with attractive performance reports on their current jobs. The company's decision makers want to be sure that they are spending this money and effort on sincere, loyal employees, the kind who might be expected to do well in the training class—in other words, those who have displayed on their jobs that enthusiastic attitude whose value I have to point out again and again.

That attitude is critical to motivating you to look for a job, critical to getting hired, and critical to getting ahead once you've landed your job. Your attitude of enthusiasm, confidence, determination, sincerity, and cheerfulness is your most important asset, both on and off the job.

If you still don't believe it, put yourself in the place of the personnel executives at the company we just talked about. Who would you hire for a job, an indifferent candidate or one who appears to really want the job? The one who shows enthusiasm, of course. In fact, might you not be inclined to choose the enthusiastic, sincere candidate over one with slightly better experience but with a lackadaisical attitude?

And who would you offer training and promotion to, the

indifferent performer or the employee who does his all-out best on his current job assignment? Obviously, you would choose the employee who had proved himself, wouldn't you?

And which employee would get "the edge" when you had one of those training class seats open? Why, the one who *asked* for it, naturally—the one who showed enthusiasm.

> ● **Rule 7 is that advancement on the job requires the same good attitude that gets you the job in the first place: enthusiasm and obvious willingness to put forth the effort. Nobody will wake you up in order to give you a promotion.**

Your enthusiastic attitude and extra effort combine with your faith in the Lord's promises to absolutely *guarantee* your success. This is not my guarantee we're talking about; it's His. Psalm 75 in *The Living Bible* promises you: "Promotion and power come from nowhere on earth, but only from God. He promotes one and deposes another" (vv. 6–7).

Be sure you understand. The jobs are there; it's a demonstrable fact and there's no denying it. Companies will do all they can to help employees acquire and improve job skills, even to the point of paying tuition at trade schools, secretarial schools, and sometimes colleges. Companies desperately want good, solid, reliable employees like you and will do anything they can to get them and to keep them happy.

THE UNEMPLOYED LACK INITIATIVE

To return to the earlier question, Why don't you have a job? Somewhere in the back of your mind might be another myth. This one involves the notion that unemployed people deserve their fate, that they lack initiative or (as my grandmother used to say) backbone. Myths like this one are insidious. They tend to become what is known in the jargon of my industrial training friend as "self-fulfilling prophecies." Basically, this means that if an unemployed person is told long enough, loud enough, and often enough that he has no gumption, he'll begin to behave as if that were true. This bitter judgment on the unemployed is embodied in the common statement, "I'd wash windows before I'd go on unemployment."

I've heard lots of people make that kind of statement, and I'll bet you have, too. Of course, it's something people only say when they're employed. The tune changes when they become the ones to lose their jobs.

If you're out of work, please promise me one thing: don't ever say anything like that once you find your job. It's cruel, and it betrays an uncharitable outlook on life.

The fact is that being out of work is different when it happens to you. You know the old joke about the difference between recession and depression. Recession is when your neighbor is out of work, and depression is when *you're* out of work.

I know only one man who really made good on a stated preference for washing windows over accepting unemployment compensation, though I never heard him make the remark itself. (He probably never would have.) He is a decent, God-loving man in a major Illinois city. The farm equipment company he worked for closed the plant, and it seemed that everybody in town had to go on unemployment insurance or welfare because the town was so dependent on that one major employer.

Well, this man really did go out and wash windows. He started humbly, offering to wash the windows of private homes around town for small amounts of money. But he always did each job conscientiously, no matter how small.

He was always on time, demonstrating still another facet of the winning attitude: *reliability*. He washed every window with as much care and precision as he formerly used on his drill press. In fact, he showed more dedication to this simple task than many people would have thought necessary.

But that kind of determination never goes unnoticed for long. Eventually, a man whose home he was working on was so impressed that he asked our friend whether he'd like to do the windows of a small office building he owned.

Other businesspeople nearby saw this window washer show up early and stay late and get the job done as well as it could be done. Increasingly, he found himself yelling his phone number down from his ladder in response to requests from below.

By the time he had the third office building contract, he had to put on a man to help him. Contract followed contract, and today he operates the largest maintenance company in Illinois outside Chicago. He's an executive now, not a window washer.

But let me tell you something else about his attitude. I called on him recently because he now uses my company to fill jobs at his company. When I showed up to take his job specifications, he shook my hand, and I couldn't help noticing that his hands were badly wrinkled and very cold. I inquired after his health and looked pointedly at his hands.

He smiled and said, "One of my men was injured slightly in a car accident yesterday. He couldn't make it in today because I told him to go to the hospital to have himself checked out thoroughly. So I went out to the building he was supposed to clean and did it myself."

I let him see my surprise and said, "But surely the people who manage the building would have understood. Surely they would have waited a few days until you could get someone to help out while your man recuperates."

"Oh, yes. That would have been easy. But we're talking about one of my oldest customers; I wouldn't let them down for anything."

I looked at my watch. "But it's only 9:00 A.M. When did you have time to do it?"

"I started at 5:00 this morning. My oldest son helped me, and we just finished a few minutes ago."

This man employs a force of thirty to fifty people, depending on the season, and here he was getting up in the middle of the night and doing with his own hands the work that had to be done.

Now that's *attitude*.

SOME WORK IS DEMEANING

His example leads us to consider one of the most destructive fallacies of all, the myth that certain kinds of work are demeaning—not good enough for you.

What's behind this myth, of course, is pride, the queen of sins. Proverb 16:18 tells us, "Pride goes before destruction, / And a haughty spirit before a fall." This is the same destructive pride of which the next verse warns us, "Better to be of a humble spirit with the lowly, / Than to divide the spoil with the proud." And those who tell us that certain kinds of work are demeaning are doing pride's work.

What happens when this fallacy becomes widespread, as it is in our society today, is that people choose to be unemployed rather than accept work that is "beneath them." And this nonsense about demeaning work makes being out of work morally, socially, and emotionally acceptable to many people.

That's where the danger lies. When the work available is thought to be demeaning, being unemployed becomes respectable. And that's a danger for the unemployed and for our society as a whole. Behavior contrary to God's plan for you should never be allowed to look respectable. It's particularly insidious for the young who need a start in life at any level of pay. Instead, this myth encourages them to spend time on the streets in preference to spending time in a job that pays a lower wage than they'd like.

The manager of the suburban Chicago airport where I used to keep my plane is a woman. She and I have become rather chummy over the years, and last year she asked me how much I would charge to recruit somebody to clean out the many private airplanes parked there. She'd been advertising for several weeks with few responses.

"People today don't want to do that kind of work," she told me, "not out here in this ritzy suburb, anyway."

I couldn't accept her comments at face value without a challenge. "Maybe if you took somebody part-time, maybe some young people after school."

"No," she said, "I asked the placement office at the college to find some applicants, but nobody ever showed up. It's like I said, people don't want to do that kind of work anymore. They think they're too good for it."

As it turned out, I didn't have to help her. One of our Chicago newspapers ran a series on jobs that nobody applies for, and the plane-cleaning job was one of the first in the series. She got plenty of applicants who came out from the city after that, and she was able to hire someone the day the story appeared.

And she was paying eight dollars an hour!

Consider the wonderful behavioral role models the Lord gave us through His own example in the Bible. One of them can be used to dispel the pride that sneakingly invades even the most pious among us: Jesus washed the feet of His disciples.

If the Lord was willing to perform such a task, who are we, you and I, to say that the tasks offered us in this world are demeaning or beneath us? Doesn't it seem to you that the Lord wants you to follow His example? How, then, can we be too good to accept whatever jobs He sees fit to put before us?

> ● **Rule 8 is that work never demeans the worker; but the worker with a negative attitude can demean his work.**

When I started my business back in 1965, I did it like many other entrepreneurs—on a shoestring. I had very little capital with which to get going. I was prepared for lean times for a while, of course, but they were leaner than I had planned. What I hadn't counted on was the peculiar method of paying fees that is standard in the recruiting industry. When we recruit somebody, the client doesn't pay our fee until at least thirty days after the candidate starts work. Many people who switch jobs have to give two weeks' notice on their current jobs before they can start new ones; and in some positions, the notice time is a month. This means that even if we'd done a million dollars' worth of business the first day we opened (which we didn't), there wouldn't be any income for at least six weeks and maybe a lot longer!

Well, sure enough, we were blessed with plenty of good business. The problem was that I had five people on my payroll and nothing coming in. By the end of the second month, I was starting to have visions of red ink in my checkbook. Still, our receivables, fees we had earned but hadn't yet collected, were so good that I knew we'd be all right if we could only hold out. I prayed for guidance on whether I should look for a partner who could put some cash in the business.

There was a restaurant in the same building where our offices were located, and I would stop in for coffee once in a while. It had to be just coffee; I certainly couldn't afford to eat lunch there in those days, much less dinner. After a while, I became friends with the owner and happened to tell him about my cash flow problems.

And that's when he offered me a job as a part-time waitress. I was delighted to take the job. I worked from 7:00 A.M. to 6:00 P.M. in my office, looking like a prosperous Michigan Avenue executive. Then I went down to the restaurant and put on my checkered apron and my little cardboard tiara and waited the snack bar part of the restaurant until the snack bar closed at 11:00 P.M.

The funny thing is that I met lots of important people while I was serving hamburgers and pouring coffee. We'd get to talking as I served, I'd explain about my "other job" in the recruiting industry, and some of those people eventually became clients of my company. You should have seen the looks on their faces when their waitress handed them her business card that said she was president of a personnel consulting company.

So, please don't ever tell me a job is "not good enough" for you. If a company president can wait tables, you can take whatever job the Lord sets aside for you.

I mostly wanted to tell that story because I thought you might enjoy it. But there's a point to it as well. I've never regretted the time I spent in the restaurant because it helped me develop a lot of insights. One of those insights involves "temporary" jobs. The nature of a temporary job, of course, is to tide you over until you find what you really want. But a temporary job can easily become permanent if your attitude toward it is right.

Here's what I mean: I was the best waitress they ever had. Not only do I say it, but the man who owned the restaurant said it, too. My tips were always better than those of the other waitresses, and most "regulars" asked to sit at my station when they came in. I only kept the job for three months, then left to concentrate on my growing personnel business. But I know for certain how it would have worked out if I'd chosen to stay. Eventually, I would have been promoted to the dinner club section of the restaurant, the fancy part with high menu prices. I would have been the first female waiter in the history of that classy restaurant. And, after a while, I would have been made maitre d'hôtel because of my attitude. Finally, if the owner ever opened another restaurant, I know he would have asked me to be his partner.

You see, I really believe that success follows a good attitude. I'm supported in that belief by secular thinkers as well as by the authority of Scripture. Napoleon esteemed attitude above all other qualities in his soldiers, saying: "The moral is to the physical as three is to one."

Read any biography of a successful businessperson. You'll see that few ever started at the top. Start anywhere you get a chance to start. But get started! Before you can get ahead on a job, you must first have the job.

The myths that there aren't enough good jobs, that jobs can't be had without a vast array of job skills, and that some jobs are demeaning must be wiped from your mind. They hold you back by convincing you that your own condition of unemployment is beyond control. They're misunderstandings about how the world really is.

But there's another class of myths that we must work on at the same time. These are the ones you create *for* yourself *about* yourself in your own mind. They have implications for your estimation of your own worth as a job applicant and, perhaps, as a person. They're fallacies you construct about yourself unthinkingly and effortlessly. But fortunately they're as easy to destroy as they are to build.

CHAPTER 4

Overcoming Self-Doubt

= ◇ =

There may be some personal and individual reasons why you feel you can't get a job. These are not the kinds of reasons that everybody shares, the kinds of misunderstandings we just talked about, but reasons why *you* in particular can't get a job—why you secretly think nobody would want to hire you.

Some of these reasons might be physical: you might feel you're too fat or too thin, too young or too old. You may have a physical handicap. Maybe you're in poor health.

Your reason might be educational: maybe you lack a high-school diploma or have poor English language skills.

Perhaps it's cultural: you're concerned that opportunity is limited because you're black or female or Hispanic.

Your reason might be historical: maybe you have a poor job record or have been fired. Maybe you haven't worked in a long time and worry about this gap in your employment history. Maybe you've been in jail and haven't been able to live down your record.

Perhaps your reason is spiritual: maybe you have a bad family situation or are a single parent. Maybe you've had a problem with drugs or alcohol. Maybe you just don't feel very good about yourself. Maybe you feel you're all alone and nobody really cares, and maybe nobody does—except the Lord.

These are some typical examples from among the many reasons I've heard during my career. And they're arranged in five broad categories: physical, educational, cultural, historical, and spiritual. The reason for this arrangement is to give you a starting place for an exercise.

This exercise begins with writing down all those reasons— all those *personal* reasons—why you haven't got a job.

Be thoughtful. Be complete. Be honest. Nobody will see what you've written down but you, so there's no reason to hold back. Think about the examples, and think about the five categories. Then close this book and write down all the reasons you can think of why you don't have a job. Don't start reading again until you have done this. In fact, it would probably be best not to read any more from this book until sometime tomorrow, after you've had a chance to sleep on the reasons and review everything you've written down. That way, you can add anything else you may think of. And it's very important to get every reason down on paper, because we're going to do something to get rid of those reasons.

So please close the book, give some serious thought to the negatives that hold you back, and start writing. Please don't go on until you've completed the exercise.

THE POWER OF THE WRITTEN WORD

There is an enormous power in the written word. Writing has been given to us as a blessing that makes the society of man possible. The spiritual value of the written word is clear when Exodus tells how God gave the law to Moses. Moses could have come down from the mountain and simply recited the law to the Israelites if God had wanted him to do only that.

But just speaking the words wasn't good enough for Moses. Exodus 24:4 tells us that "Moses wrote all the words of the LORD." And the spoken word wasn't good enough for God, either. "Come up to Me on the mountain and be there," He said to Moses, "and I will give you tablets of stone, and the law and commandments *which I have written,* that you may teach them" (Exod. 24:12, emphasis added).

Mount Sinai was smoking and quaking, and the air was filled with trumpet blasts and thunder. It's fair to say that the Israelites would have remembered any messages they heard under such circumstances. They wouldn't have needed it to be written down. But both Moses and God took the trouble to *write* the law. The power of the written word surpasses that of the spoken word.

That's why you wrote all those negatives that seem to prevent you from getting a job. Merely thinking about them isn't enough. Reciting them out loud is much better. But the power of the written word can only be used if you commit your thoughts to writing. Nothing will organize and clarify your thoughts better than writing them down.

Writing your ideas makes them concrete and allows you to manipulate them. It allows you to become the master of the ideas the words represent. And the negative ideas you have about work, about employers, and about yourself are all that prevent you from getting a job. In effect, they're more myths. Only this time, they're fallacies that you've told yourself *about* yourself. And this makes them the vilest untruths of all. They sully the enthusiastic attitude toward life that employers find so appealing.

You must manipulate those negatives, you must become their master, in order to get rid of them.

The second part of the exercise is easier than the first, and more fun, too. Take your pencil or, better yet, a black felt-tip marker, and scratch out the negatives you've written down. They're lies you've told yourself about yourself, so don't be bashful; attack those negatives with vigor. Scratch them out until you've worn a hole in the paper if that helps. Destroy them, obliterate them completely until you're satisfied that they no longer exist in the real world but only in your mind.

This may not work completely the first time you do it. What you're trying to do is to clean house, to evict those negatives, those lies about yourself, from your mind. They may not want to go. They've been in there for a long time and feel that they have a long-term lease. Nonetheless, you can evict them if you really want to. The way to ensure it is to do this exercise every day until you get a job. Get up in the morning and write those negatives down. Then scratch them out gleefully. Destroy them. Make them go away. Very soon, perhaps immediately, you will begin to feel good as you destroy the negatives. And that's what the exercise is all about.

If this exercise seems a little peculiar to you, that's only because you've never done it before. I've been assigning this exercise to attendees of my job seminars since the seminars began. And I can give you my word that the exercise is effective. So don't be embarrassed, don't think the exercise is silly; do it with a ready heart. Just try it and you'll see that it works. You'll feel better every time you destroy those negatives. And as you destroy them, as you clean them out of your mind, there will be a void left that you can fill with positives.

But remember that you have to do the exercise every day, writing the negatives down and then happily, joyfully, confidently destroying them.

Actually, we have a sound basis for this rather peculiar behavior. The strength provided through manipulation of the written word has long been recognized. In Jerusalem, for example, devout Jews pray at the Western Wall of the Temple. But they do more. They write their messages to God on little slips of paper that they then insert into cracks in the Wall.

Buddhists have little machines that spin rapidly like electric fans. They write their prayers on these cylinders, or "prayer wheels," and believe that every spin of the wheel sends their prayers to Buddha. A Christian would suggest that they've lost all the personality of prayer in their quest for efficiency, but the example remains valid in one respect: there are ways to deal with the written word, ways that give you mastery over what the word represents.

The Egyptians used to write down the name of some quality they particularly admired, such as courage or confidence, and then eat the piece of papyrus on which the word was written. You don't have to go that far! Just writing down your negatives and then destroying those negatives are adequate to give you the feeling of mastery over them.

A curious thing begins to happen when you've done the exercise a few times. You begin to discover that some of the negatives about which you were so concerned really weren't all that important in the first place.

This happened to a young man who called on me a few years ago to interview in connection with a recruiting assignment on which my company was working. He struck me as being altogether acceptable for the job except that he kept apologizing for his lack of a high-school diploma. The job involved order processing for an auto parts warehouse. The ability to read and write English was essential, of course, as were a friendly manner and a pleasant telephone voice. None of these qualities require advanced education, do they? But he went on and on explaining how his parents were poor, how he had to quit school to help support his brothers and sisters, and so forth.

He didn't get the job. He was just too sensitive about this negative idea, and it showed in his attitude. Still, he seemed to be a pleasant and sincere young man, so I took a coffee break and explained the exercise to him. At first he couldn't bring himself to believe that anything so simple could be as effective as I claimed. But, inasmuch as he had nothing to lose, he tried it.

Every day he would write on a big yellow tablet: "I can't get anywhere without a 'sheepskin.'" Then he would scratch it out, timidly at first, then with more and more gusto. After a couple of weeks, he came to understand that his lack of formal education was more important to him than it was to anybody else.

He also came to understand that as long as he confined his job search to occupations where formal education was not a strict requirement, he was on a level playing field with the other applicants. One of his insights, he told me, was that college graduates were not applying for the kinds of customer-service jobs he wanted anyway. The competition he so feared didn't even exist! This insight caused my young friend to realize that his worth was more than could be represented by a piece of paper attesting to academic attainments. It caused him to think about himself until he discovered that as one of God's children, he had a worth and a dignity that would let him hold his head high in proper self-respect.

Within a couple of weeks, he had a job with the telephone company. The last time I had occasion to speak with him, he was a supervisor in the customer-service department dealing with commercial accounts, and he seemed happy with his career.

There are scores of stories just like this that I could tell you, stories about people who discovered that some of the negatives they feared were just shadows. And by writing your fears out and then symbolically destroying them, you, too, will get a better perspective on who you are. You will also get a better perspective on those factors in your life that *really* deserve your attention.

Now let's suppose that you go through the exercise and list, say, a half-dozen negatives. Every day you scratch them out. Soon, you come to understand that most of them are not really very important and you don't even bother to list them anymore because you've mastered them. You've found out those lies, and you've seen them wither to nothingness.

But maybe there's one negative thought that just won't go away, no matter how diligently you scratch it out. Maybe it's something really serious that limits your horizons and saps your ambition. Maybe it's some dreadful problem from your past.

You have to live with that problem. But you don't have to live with the shame and fear that often accompany really severe problems. God has given us wonderful mental abilities. With His help, and by using those abilities, you can actually turn those really important negatives into positives. You can turn your lemons into lemonade.

CHAPTER 5

Turning Personal Negatives
into Positives

$= \Diamond =$

You'll be surprised at how easily many of the negative feelings you have go away when you recognize them and symbolically scratch them out of your life. But what can you do about those mental drawbacks that are of such magnitude that recognizing them is not enough to eliminate them? An example that is, sadly, becoming more common all the time is that of the single parent with dependent children at home. For many women, this seems to be an insurmountable barrier to getting hired.

They're afraid that a prospective employer will wonder what will happen when those children get sick; will the single mother stay away from work to take care of her youngsters? What about all the other chunks of time that are needed to raise children: trips to the dentist, visits to school, and the like? Will those family needs, important as everyone recognizes they are, show up on the job as poor attendance?

Single mothers are afraid that the employer will secretly wonder: Can she take care of her children and still show up consistently for work? And single mothers are absolutely right to fear that. Such doubt in the interviewer's mind will make it difficult for the single parent to get hired.

Unless that negative factor is turned into a positive one.

If being a single parent with the responsibility of children is your big barrier to full-time employment, turn it into a positive factor by letting the interviewer know the steps you've taken to handle your responsibility. For example, find a day-care center for your children, and identify it to the interviewer. Even if you haven't any money to pay for day care until you get a job, you can visit a few centers in your neighborhood and arrange for one to accept your children after you've found a job. If you have relatives or friends who are prepared to share the responsibility, identify that fact to the interviewer as well. If your mother has offered to help you, let the interviewer know how close she lives and how you can easily take your children to her before the work day begins. If you're blessed with good health for your children and you have seldom needed to miss work in order to tend their illnesses, let that be known. Tell the interviewer that the children have their medical, dental, and optometry appointments in the evenings so that you won't have to take time off from work.

Since your handling of the situation shows your maturity and responsibility, since it gives you greater esteem in the eyes of the interviewer, why fear it? The case of dependent children at home has a potential effect on work habits, and you know the interviewer has to ask about this area of your life eventually. So why not get it out in the open? Why not beat him to the punch? Why not say, "Mr. Interviewer, I know you're concerned that I have two youngsters at home. I'd like to tell you how I plan to handle their needs in such a way as not to intrude on my work habits"? By bringing the subject up yourself, you show you've got nothing to hide. This approach can't possibly hurt you. In fact, it can only improve your standing with the interviewer.

Do you see what all this is leading up to? You have taken a negative (the potential of absence from work due to family considerations) and turned it into a positive by showing how well you handle responsibility and how well you are able to organize your life. You present the image of a mature, well-organized adult with planned procedures at your fingertips.

> ● **Rule 9 is that employers are not reluctant to hire somebody with obligations that could be viewed negatively, but they *are* reluctant to hire somebody who doesn't know how to handle those obligations.**

You've turned a potential negative into a positive. And you don't have to write it down any longer on your list of negatives to be scratched out of your life. You'll put it on the list of another exercise you'll be doing, a list of positives for which thanks is due to God (more on that in the next chapter).

CONSEQUENCES OF FAILURE TO TURN NEGATIVES INTO POSITIVES

Let's consider now what happens if you *don't* turn your negatives into positives, if you let those negatives get the upper hand. The result is that the negative thought can start to control your attitude. This happens if you fail to deal with the shame or fear of the negative thought through the use of disciplines like the crossing-out exercise. It happens if you fail to confront the negative and turn it into a positive with good planning. And it certainly happens if you try to pretend the negative doesn't exist. These are the worst things a job hunter can do. An example may make clear the way in which negative thoughts can become obsessive.

When I first interviewed George, I observed that he was fortyish, well spoken and well mannered, and apparently cheerful. When I greeted him, he shook my hand firmly and

confidently. He had an open smile and met my eyes unflinch-
ingly. He was dressed neatly in a conservative style that gave
him an air of competence. His manner was relaxed and cordial, yet professional. He took the seat I offered him and gave
the appearance of being calm yet attentive.

Incidentally, notice that I haven't said anything so far about
his background and qualifications. Yet you've probably concluded already that I was favorably impressed with George.
Notice the things I commented about above. They indicate a
good attitude, don't they?

I looked over the application George had prepared for me. I
learned that he was also college educated and had plenty of
sales experience in the electronics industry. The job I needed
to fill was the position of sales manager for an electronics
distributor, and George was beginning to look like a good potential candidate.

As I reviewed the application with him, I admired the poise
with which he answered my questions and clarified things I
didn't fully understand about his background. His relaxed,
confident manner marked him as a skillful communicator, an
important attribute in a salesperson.

Then I came to a gap in the application, a period beginning
about a year previously during which George seemed not to
have worked. I asked him to explain the gap, and for the first
time he began to get a little nervous. He mumbled something I
didn't catch, and I had to ask him to repeat. He never did
answer my question satisfactorily, and he never regained his
poise.

The interview ended a few minutes later with George acting
very tense. He seemed frightened to talk about something in
his past, and I had no idea what it was. But his attitude had
decayed to the point that he seemed overcome by some sort of

shame. He was stuttering and stammering continually by the end of the interview, and our conversation had ceased to be productive. I felt very sorry for him and sympathized with his discomfort.

Needless to say, George did not get the job.

Several months later I was interviewing for another company that needed an electronics salesperson. The receptionist ushered in the first applicant, and I found myself shaking hands with George!

He had a big, confident smile in place when he walked in. But it melted like ice in the August sun the instant he recognized me. He became embarrassed again, just as he had during our first meeting. He offered to leave rather than waste my time interviewing for a job where, as he said, "you won't give me a chance."

I had allotted forty-five minutes for the interview and the next candidate hadn't arrived yet, so I asked George to have a seat.

"Look," he said, "I don't want to waste your time."

"My time is your time," I said. "Why don't we talk a bit, get to know each other?"

George took a chair and sat on the edge of it as though he was going to jump up and run out of the office at any second.

"The problem is," he said, "you're going to ask me about my 'missing year.' Just like the other interviewers I've talked to these last months. None of you will ever let me live it down."

"George, I don't even know what you're trying to 'live down,'" I said. "You won't tell me. And I'll bet you haven't told any other interviewers, either."

"You're right," he said after a minute. "I get embarrassed when the subject comes up. You see," he sort of gulped, "I'm an alcoholic. It got so bad that I had to be institutionalized in a detoxification center. That was about the time my wife left me; she took the kids, too, of course.

"Then when I got out, my boss fired me; said he didn't need any 'boozers' in his company. So I haven't had a job or a family in all that time, and it's hard for me to admit all these problems. I'm sure you can appreciate my embarrassment."

"I'm not so sure I can, George," I answered. "Might it be that your embarrassment is overemphasized, that you've taken steps to correct your past problems? For example, I'll bet you've joined Alcoholics Anonymous, haven't you?"

"Oh yes—an outstanding institution. They've helped me a lot. I haven't had a drink in over a year now."

"So when you said you were an alcoholic, you were wrong, weren't you? You're a *recovering* alcoholic, and that's quite different, isn't it?"

"Well," he said, "I suppose it is. But I haven't worked in all that time. Won't an interviewer hold that against me?"

"How have you been living?" I asked. "On your savings?"

"No, my wife took everything out of the bank when she left. I haven't been sitting around doing nothing, of course. I sell shoes part-time. But it's not the profession for which I was trained, so I don't count it."

Here was a man who had his life turned completely upside down and had managed to survive. In fact, he told me that he was so good at selling shoes that the manager of the store kept asking him to come to work full-time. George only declined because he wanted to look for work in electronics, which was the business he knew best and which he truly enjoyed.

He'd conquered alcoholism, one of the most insidious diseases the devil has ever thought up. He'd lost his family and all his savings but was persevering in spite of it all. And he'd been able to make a living at a job for which he'd never had the chance to prepare.

What did he have to be ashamed of? On the contrary, he had every reason to be glad he had found the strength to overcome his problems and to feel hopeful about a future without those problems. His *real* problem was that he was looking at his experiences negatively instead of positively.

"You know, George," I told him, "alcoholism is a common disease among salespeople. Some even consider it an occupational hazard. Do you think companies worry about the problem?"

"I know they do," he replied. "But I guess there's no way for them to be sure that the problem won't crop up, even in their best employees."

"Tell me, do you think *you* will ever take a drink again?"

"Me?" He was startled. "No way. Never again. Not after what I've been through."

"Would you be ashamed to explain to an employer why he'll never have to worry about that particular problem with you?"

"Well, when you put it that way. . . ."

"That's the *only* way to put it, George. And at the same time, think about whether you respect other recovering alcoholics."

"Why, of course I do! It takes courage to kick that habit, even if I say so myself. I don't want to sound boastful, but you have to admire somebody who makes it."

"I agree with you, George. I respect somebody who's conquered a problem more than somebody who's never been tested. It's like that famous Bible verse, Luke 15:7, 'I say to you that likewise there will be more joy in heaven over one sinner who repents than over ninety-nine just persons who need no repentance.' And you know what? Almost everyone else will feel exactly the same way."

> ● **Rule 10 is that if you're thinking about a really big negative in your past, the interviewer is thinking about it, too. You'll never hide it from a good interviewer. So get it out in the open and turn it into a positive.**

I might as well tell you that George didn't get that job, either, Rule 10 notwithstanding. He simply wasn't ready yet. He had to learn to live with his past. He had to learn to handle his "big negative." He knew that the Lord understood what had happened to him, and he wasn't worried about that anymore. But he had to learn that his fellow man would be understanding, too.

You're probably prepared to forgive anybody who has wronged you and who wants to mend his ways. Certainly if you're a Christian, you should have a forgiving nature. Doesn't it seem reasonable that other people will afford you the same privilege? Don't you think they'll be prepared to be considerate about mistakes in your past, to give you another chance—especially when you display all that you've learned from a mistake and let everyone know how it's made you better? People are more understanding than you may realize.

By the way, don't be too concerned about George. He did some of the exercises and came to a job seminar. He found an electronics sales job a short time later and is now doing very nicely indeed. I'd like to ask him to speak at one of our seminars if I can ever catch him between his important business trips.

TURNING AROUND EVEN THE BIGGEST NEGATIVES

Praise God that most of us have less severe problems than George. But always bear in mind that some people have greater problems.

A young man who stayed around after one of our earliest seminars and asked to speak to me privately is a case in point. He told me that he wanted to accept what I'd said about turning negatives into positives, but he just couldn't bring himself to believe it. We prayed together for faith, and then he told me his story.

He said that his negative was so big that he didn't have to write it down to recognize it. He said that his big negative was never far from his mind, that it was with him always.

He was thirty-two years old and had no job history at all; he'd never been employed! To make matters worse, he'd been in jail for a few months for burglary. He told me his future was hopeless.

Remember what the negative images you create about yourself in your own mind do to you. They make you ready to accept being out of work. They give you a neatly packaged reason not to look for a job. They take some of the sting out of being unemployed. I wasn't about to agree with this young man that his situation was hopeless; there's no such thing.

Fortunately, even after the shambles his life had been, this young man clearly wanted to turn himself around. I could hear it in his voice, and I could see it in his eyes. But he had to learn to deal with his important negatives and turn them into positives.

It's not commonly known, but several organizations exist to help rehabilitated offenders. They tend to be local organizations, not national ones. The way to contact one of them is to check with the penal authorities in your area. The organization I occasionally work through in Chicago is run by a former offender. And thank God that some of those who have been in prison remember what it's like when they get out and resume productive lives.

These self-help groups are usually called "networks," and they exist, usually on an informal basis, to help anyone with a particular job-hunting concern. For example, numerous women's networks share information about employers who are not prone to the bias that sometimes is found against women in business.

If you're concerned that being black or Hispanic or female is a big drawback to your success, you probably need to do the scratching-out exercise some more; those characteristics tend to be less of a barrier to employment than they once were. But if you want to feel you're maximizing your efforts, join a network; just ask your friends, and you'll be surprised at how many referrals you get.

We used a network for the young man who'd been in prison, and he did indeed find a job. He's now a "solid citizen." (To make the story even better, he's also become a Christian.) But there's an interesting sidelight to his story that illustrates the concept of making positives out of negatives.

At one time, he'd organized a motorcycle club; nothing criminal, he assured me, but a pretty rough-looking bunch of people nonetheless. One of the interviews that we arranged through the network, the one that eventually resulted in a job offer, was with a major car dealer in Chicago, and the subject of the motorcycle club came up during the interview. The owner of the dealership later called me and told me he thought my friend had good supervisory potential. He said that anybody who could run a motorcycle club could certainly handle his repair department! It's just another instance of how a negative can be turned into a positive and of how forgiving employers can be *if* the applicant has changed the ways that led to that negative in the first place.

But by far the most inspiring stories of all about turning negatives into positives are those that involve the handicapped. It's a wonder to see all the people who have found the courage to persevere and conquer their handicaps. It makes us conscious of a great blessing, the blessing that we live in a time and place in which diversity of opportunity allows people to work and find professional fulfillment in occupations to which their handicaps are irrelevant.

I could tell you about a big bank in downtown Chicago that has long had a policy of hiring the handicapped in such job positions. If you could tour their facilities, as I had the pleasure of doing recently, you'd see people in wheelchairs talking on the phone and using computer terminals to find account information for customers. Their inability to walk couldn't be less important to the job they're doing.

I could tell you about a department populated largely by hearing-impaired and speech-impaired persons who write computer programs; the computer can't tell that they have a handicap.

I could tell you about two brothers who work at that institution, both blind since birth. One is blessed with great intellectual gifts; through his own efforts and attitude and with the grace of God, he made it through law school and is now a corporate attorney there. His younger brother has not been given the same intellectual gifts but has received abundant gifts of personality. He enjoys his work in the training department. And I could tell you about the tears of joy and bountiful glory that surround them every Christmas Eve when the two brothers minister in the bank's Christmas choir; one plays the organ while the other sings solo carols in a magnificent tenor voice. And nobody who hears them thinks about their blindness.

But I don't have to tell you about all that. Turn on the news any night and you'll hear about people with no legs who complete the marathon in wheelchairs, sightless children who learn to play baseball, and the Special Olympics for youngsters on whom God has not bestowed the favors of perfect intellectual health.

If you want to learn how to turn negatives into positives, how to "turn lemons into lemonade," as I always tell attendees at our job seminars, watch these people. They demonstrate that it's better to work with what you have rather than to regret what you do not have. Study their attitudes. Then "go thou and do likewise."

CHAPTER 6

What You've Got Going for You

= ◇ =

A few months ago, while in New York on business, I ran into an old friend in the coffee shop of the hotel where we both happened to be staying. We shared a table for breakfast, and I noticed he wasn't looking his usual dapper, cheerful self. I thought he looked distraught, haggard even, and I let him see my concern over his state.

"I'm working on the biggest deal of my life," he said. "I've put everything I've got into it. And I'm worried that it might not go my way. If it doesn't, I don't know what I'll do."

"Oh, come on," I said. "You've worked on big deals before. This can't be so bad."

"But if it doesn't turn out, I'll lose everything. I'll have nothing left—nothing left to live for."

I was upset by his remarks. He wasn't the type of man to say such things. There's *always* something left to live for. What he'd said was so out of character, I decided he must have a really serious problem.

"Have you had a crisis of faith?" I asked. I'd always known him to be a deeply religious man. I couldn't think of anything else that would justify the bitterness of his words and his tone.

"No, no. It's business; nothing to do with the Lord."

I wasn't so sure about *that*, but I let it pass for the moment.

"I'm sure things will work out right for you," I said. "But

even if they didn't, you'd still have your family, wouldn't you? They'd still love you."

"Yes, of course, Carol and the kids would stick by me through anything. But I'd be broke! I'd be finished!"

I decided to try a different approach. "You have your health, youth, energy," I said. "You're only—what—late thirties? Even if you lost everything. . . ."

"Don't even think of it!" he groaned.

"Even if you lost everything," I went on, "you could still start again."

We went on that way all through breakfast: me reminding him of his blessings, him acknowledging them but still complaining.

Over coffee, I suggested he make a list—not a list of negatives to be destroyed and eliminated, but a list of positives to be nurtured and cherished.

He'd already assured me that the three most important aspects of life were secure: faith, family, and health. How much more did he need? By forgetting all the wonderful gifts in his life, he'd lost sight of what comes first; he'd let his priorities get out of order.

But all our earthly priorities have been neatly ordered for us in Scripture. How the Lord must have laughed when He chose a former tax collector, one who had been dedicated to worldly possessions, to record the order as one of His most moving teachings in Matthew 6:25, 32–33:

> Therefore I say to you, do not worry about your life, what you will eat or what you will drink; nor about your body, what you will put on. Is not life more than food and the body more than clothing? . . .
>
> For after all these things the Gentiles seek. For your heavenly Father knows that you need all these things.

*But seek first the kingdom of God and His righteousness,
and all these things shall be added to you* (emphasis added).

The point is that it's easy to take our blessings for granted.
It's easy to see the negatives in our lives and ignore all the
positives. Even people of faith can fall into this trap, as my
friend did. Sometimes it's necessary to stop and take stock of
what God has given us instead of worrying about what He has
chosen not to give us yet.

Which brings us to our next exercise. Make a list, just as
you did before. Only this time list all the positive things in
your life, not the negatives. Think of all the reasons why you
are a person of worth and value and of all those people who
would give testimony to that fact.

You know, when we get busy with the world we forget to
count up all those who love and respect us. We get accustomed to our blessings, we take them for granted. But if you
want the happy, winning attitude, take a close look at your
blessings. Just like my friend in New York, you may find you
have more to be positive about than you usually take the time
to consider.

And while you're making the list, why not make it a prayer
of thanksgiving?

Now, go ahead and start your list. Just like before, be
thoughtful, be complete, be honest. Please don't go on until
you've created at least a rough draft of your list.

THE POWER OF RECOUNTING YOUR BLESSINGS

Quite a task, wasn't it? I know you wrote down the things
we've already mentioned: faith in the Lord, love of family and
friends, health. Let me mention another one that I certainly

hope you wrote down. If you missed it, that's okay. Write it down the next time you make your list.

What "next time"? The list of positives is just like the list of negatives; you have to write it every day until you get a job. As more blessings continue to come to mind because you're consciously looking for them, your list will grow.

But remember to do the exercise every day. When you go on a job interview, you want to have those positives fresh in your mind. The day will come when you notice that your positives list is getting bigger and your negatives list is getting shorter. That will be a very happy day. It'll be the day when all the list making really starts to pay off.

The positive I hope you didn't miss is so basic, so fundamental, so much an ingrained part of our lives that I can understand how you might not have thought about it.

We live in America.

I don't have to tell you all the usual reasons that's a blessing. You know those well enough. We all do. But for purposes of this exercise, consider America and all the other free democracies in the context of a place to work. America is a veritable fountain of jobs, a great engine of employment in a world of subsistence work or no work at all. In no other place have so many people grown to affluence from the humblest of beginnings. America is a gusher of opportunity. This book would be useless anywhere else. Only in our free democracies has God provided that *every* citizen can raise himself up. And this most definitely includes *you!*

It includes you no matter who you are. A little earlier, I suggested some commonly held negative ideas for you to think about. Then we looked at some of them in detail and saw right through them. But we ignored one important one, and it's time now to make up for that deficiency by relating this so-called drawback to our great country.

Some job seekers would insist that being members of a minority group is the reason they can't get hired.

Hogwash.

It's my business to know the job market and the laws that affect employment. Groups that formerly were the objects of job discrimination are no longer so. Where else have laws been passed that assure freedom of opportunity?

There's a diabolical remark that's designed to make minority group members feel depressed and negative about their prospects. Whenever we're told that opportunity is now more open than it was, that members of minority groups have come a long way, somebody always reminds us that "there's a long way yet to go."

It's another of those insidious remarks that cause us to take our eyes off our blessings. It's the old story again of a half glass of water. The person who loves his negatives and doesn't want to relinquish their comforts insists that the glass is half-empty. The person who cherishes the positive aspects of life will know that it's half-full.

Let depressing speculations be the property of the sociologists. You have to have positive thoughts if you want your attitude to be a winning one. If you're a member of a minority group, think not about how far your group has to go, but about how far you've come. You can't afford to harbor thoughts any less positive than that, not if you're determined to be successful in job hunting.

WE'RE ALL GIFTED

In this chapter, we haven't talked about negatives that need to be turned into positives. We've talked about those blessings already in your life that are inherently good. Everybody has some, and every one of them has value. Maybe, for example, you have the strength and vigor of youth. Then again, maybe you have the wisdom and prudence that come with maturity. It has to be one of those two, right?

Maybe you're compassionate and would be perfect for a people-oriented job. Maybe you have a passive personality; you're a good listener, which is an indispensable gift for any job requiring analysis. On the other hand, maybe you're assertive, blessed to be what all the want ads clamor for: a "self-starter," an "eager beaver," a "go-getter." These qualities are much in demand, as you'll see for yourself when you study the want ads.

People are paid for the value they bring to their jobs. Every person has an employment value that is the total of the gifts given to him or her by God. Find the value of your gifts by consciously looking at them and thanking Him for them every day.

The point is, you may not know how *really good* you are unless you think about it searchingly and deliberately. And that's why you'll do the exercise every day. As you become more aware of the blessings God has already given you, you'll become more confident about yourself. You'll come to understand that you're a winner! Not pridefully, but with the feeling of satisfaction and security that "Somebody up there likes me." Otherwise why would He already have given you all those gifts before you even asked for them?

● **Rule 11 is that God has already given you more good things than you could ever have thought of asking for. Count them and be amazed.**

THE IMPORTANCE OF ATTITUDE

The fact that you're going to ask the Lord to take the oars of your job-seeking boat doesn't mean that you can sit back and enjoy the ride. There are a lot of mechanical aspects associated with getting hired, and we'll review them and look at some examples. You'll have to prepare a resume. You'll want to pick a group of realistic targets. You'll also need to pay special attention to proper interviewing, because the interview is "make or break" time. The best job skills in the world won't help you unless you interview the way you're going to learn to interview in this book.

All these mechanical aspects are important, and we'll certainly treat them accordingly. But for right now, remember once again that your *attitude* is the starting point for all your future success. You must accept this fact and get your attitude in shape *now*. To effectively carry out all the mechanical aspects of job hunting, which will take up most of the rest of this book, you'll need that attitude. With that in mind, this might be a good time to summarize what we've talked about up to this point.

Companies desperately want to hire employees with an attitude that shows enthusiasm, confidence, determination, sincerity, and cheerfulness. I call this a Christian attitude since no one should have a better attitude than Christians, but anyone who genuinely displays such an approach to life and work will be in demand.

Work is emotionally important to all of us. Because of the natural depression that accompanies being out of work, it takes deliberate effort to be "up," to let your attitude show. Many false stories about job seeking make that natural depression even more severe.

But those false stories, those "myths" as we called them, can be exploded if you look at the facts carefully. Your mood is largely under your own control, and one way to calm and improve your mood is to recognize fallacies when you hear them.

Most of the drawbacks that you perceive to your getting hired are fictions of your own depressed state of mind and can be eliminated. Some drawbacks, however, have greater substance and can be perceived by others as well as by you. You can turn them into positives by planning and effort and through grace. And the blessings that already exist in your life far outweigh the drawbacks anyway, if you only stop and think about them.

Now I suggest that you stop reading for a while. It's important that you be ready to receive the information in the rest of this book. It's "recipe" information, and it's vital that you follow the recipe exactly.

Much of what we talk about will require personal effort on your part. You have to understand that you already have a full-time job, even if you think you're unemployed. Your full-time job is "job hunter." And being a job hunter is the kind of job that takes a lot of work and even more faith.

So if you think you might need some additional attitude recovery before going on, close the book. Pray first for guidance. Then do the exercises again. List the negatives that work against a successful job hunt for you and wipe them out. Turn substantial negatives into positives by examining all that you've learned from them and how they've made you better. Then count up all the positives God has already given you for free and be absolutely amazed.

When you feel you're ready, we'll move on.

PART II
HOW TO DO IT:
AN INSIDER'S TECHNIQUES

CHAPTER 7

The Truth about Resumes

$= \Diamond =$

Some of the activities performed during your job search require a modest and reasonable investment of your time, although a trip to the business section of your local bookstore or library might lead you to believe otherwise. The documents and techniques associated with your job hunt have become the stuff of a vast number of books. These documents and techniques include

—the resume,

—the introductory, or "cover," letter,

—the follow-up, and

—interviewing techniques that range from dressing for success to using verbal and physical ploys to get "power" over an interviewer.

I deliberately used the word *vast* when describing the number of books on these subjects. Our modern, achievement-oriented, corporate society has spawned a whole new industry of self-help books on how to get a job. Visit your local bookstore and be bewildered by the number of titles on the same subject. The how-to-get-a-job publishing industry has made a mountain—no, a mountain *range*—out of an anthill.

Why are so many books needed for a simple subject?

It's because the personnel specialists writing those books are sincere in wanting to give you your money's worth. They try to tell you everything they know as experts in their field. They strive for a completeness and perfection that no human being can ever attain. In fact, they try to tell you more than you need or care to know.

There's a danger in all that excess information. You might get the erroneous impression from the size and number of these books that job hunting is complex and forbidding. You might become so bedeviled by all the detail to be mastered that you don't know where to begin. Being unable to reach the state of near perfection implied by the books, you begin to doubt your adequacy for the job market. You become disheartened at the task before you; this, of course, depresses your attitude.

Worst of all, you may spend so much time analyzing and trying to perfect your resume, your attire, and your interviewing style that you don't get around to arranging interviews for yourself until much precious time has been wasted. As a result, the instructions given in those books, although well intentioned, are frequently so complex and time consuming that trying to follow them all may do more harm than good.

It's not my purpose to attack those how-to books. Indeed, the collection of them in my office is not only large but well thumbed. Many of those books have much to say. That's my problem with them: they have "much" to say. Too much, I suspect.

I'll admit that you might need extraspecial efforts to nurture your career path if you've been given the many gifts to enable you to work at a high corporate level. In that case, by all means use the many fine books and services available. But most of us, and I include myself, get by very well on common sense, truthfulness, and tact. For the majority of us job seekers, everything else falls under the heading of "bells and whistles"—fine if you can afford the time and money, but hardly essential.

Take the subject of resumes, for instance. Last week, I vis-

ited an enormous bookstore in downtown Chicago for the purpose of sampling the population of books about resumes and
related subjects. I counted *twenty-two* in the paperback section on the lower level. I found *seventeen more* in the hard-
cover section upstairs. The man behind the counter offered to
help me, although the way he'd been staring suspiciously at
my note taking made me wonder whether he thought I was
some kind of spy from another bookstore.

When I told him I was interested in books on resume preparation, he smiled and told me the ones on display were only
the recent crop. If I wanted some of the "older" ones, those
published more than about a year ago or so, he could order
them for me. He had a big reference book with more titles on
the subject than I cared to count.

My concern about all this competing information is that it
makes your simple task look like a burden—such a burden, in
fact, that it even prevents some people from looking for a job,
at least for a while. I've actually encountered people who have
been out of work for extended periods and haven't had any
interviews during those months. When asked what they've
been doing all that time, most of them answer, "I've been
getting my resume together."

Don't be misled! Preparing a resume is far simpler than it
looks. In fact, it's so simple that every job seeker should have
a resume. You'll share my opinion when you learn what a
resume *really* is (as opposed to what you may *think* it is) and
when you see how easy it is to prepare one. But let me caution
you: never let the task of preparing a resume interfere with
your task of interviewing.

● **Rule 12 is that a resume will never get
you a job. A resume only gets you an interview. An interview is what gets you a job.**

WHY EVERYONE NEEDS A RESUME

You might argue that you don't need a resume because you're not looking for the kind of job that requires one. Of course, you're aware that for any kind of office job or other white-collar work, a resume has become essential at all levels. But in certain occupations, those usually classified as blue-collar (such as factory work, trucking, construction, and so forth), resumes are generally expected only at the executive levels. Nonetheless, a resume is a good thing for you to have no matter what kind of work you're seeking. There are three reasons for this.

First, mailing a resume is often the only way to respond to an ad. Employers in growing numbers continue to ask you to mail your resume as a means of making initial contact with you. Certainly, your good attitude requires you to cooperate with a prospective employer's wishes. It may be that you're in one of those industries where an interviewer is unlikely to ask you for a resume. But if you find out about the job through a newspaper ad, you may have no way to get to see that interviewer unless you have a resume to mail. Besides, it never hurts to be prepared, does it?

The second reason is that the resume is helpful to you whether you actually hand it to a prospective employer or whether you just have it with you while filling out an application form. Here's why: it's easy to forget the details of your past. You remember where you worked most recently, of course, but how about the first job you ever had? What were the dates? You certainly remember where you went to school. But if your family moved around a lot, as mine did, you may have several different names and sets of dates to try to remember. If you carry your resume with you, being asked to fill out an application form will never be intimidating.

The third reason may be the most important one. Remember when I told you that the very best jobs are not advertised? Very often they are known to people who currently work at the companies where the jobs are available. In other words, some of the very best jobs are known to friends of yours who work at those companies.

Now this ought to give you a bright idea. The best thing to do when you're looking for work is to *let all your friends and family know about it*. This is known as "networking" (as distinct from using a "network," one of those organizations such as we discussed in Chapter 5 that helps people who have a particular job-hunting concern). Networking is the best way to get the best job, and I'll have lots more to say about it later.

Therefore, don't be shy and don't be embarrassed. If your places were reversed, you'd be pleased to be able to help out a friend or relative, wouldn't you? They feel the same way and will be happy to put your name forward once they know you're "looking." But you have to let them know first, don't you?

When you tell your friends, your relatives, and everybody else you know that you're looking for a job, one of the first things they're likely to say is, "Give me a copy of your resume." Therefore, it's wise to have a copy with you at *all* times; the Lord might (and often does) provide a networking contact for you even at a social function.

THE GENERIC JOB APPLICATION

It might help you get started if you think of your resume as a generic job application form. If there were some kind of universal job application form that every company in the world used, you wouldn't need a resume. Because there is no such form, you help employers by preparing your own universal job application form. We just call it a resume, that's all. It's a simple document that answers only three questions: what have you been doing so far, where have you been doing it, and when?

Now I'll let you in on another secret, one of those tips of the trade that insiders in the recruiting business know. There are only two qualities that are *critical* to a good resume: accuracy and neatness.

Accuracy means only that you account honestly and completely for all of your time. If you were unemployed or otherwise unoccupied for any length of time longer than about three months, that time must be accounted for. There's a very simple way to account for it regardless of circumstances, and I'll tell you about it later in this chapter.

Neatness is an obvious requirement. In many cases, your first contact with an interviewer will be through your resume. Your resume, therefore, is the very first indication of your *attitude*. There are some simple, inexpensive ways to ensure neatness, which we'll also talk about soon.

The last part of the secret is that we interviewers regard favorably a candidate who keeps his resume *simple*. In fact, the "bare bones" approach is best for most people. Speaking as a professional recruiter, I can tell you that one of the biggest mistakes most applicants make is to use an overblown, over-prepared, and overly expensive resume. If an applicant has the qualifications, he still gets the interview, of course. But I certainly wish I could get back all the time and money that are wasted on overdoing resumes.

Please don't try to "sell yourself" to me with your resume. We recruiters have to look at resumes all day. If you were a recruiter, how do you think you would feel about an applicant whose resume was the 100th one you'd read that day and was so complicated you had to read it ten times just to get the sense of it? Do you think you'd feel very good about that applicant?

● **Rule 13 is that a resume is no different from all other forms of written business communication: the simpler, the better.**

So far, it sounds like a snap, doesn't it? A resume is a generic job application form. It only answers three questions: what, where, and when. The only two important qualities it has are accuracy and neatness. And the simpler it is, the better it is. In fact, it sounds like it's too easy, doesn't it? There must be a catch.

Wrong! There isn't any catch. The preparation of your resume is just as straightforward as I've made it sound. It must be done with great care, of course, since it gives an interviewer his first impression of you. But it's no more complicated conceptually than what I've told you. And the same is true for all the other techniques you'll be learning: the whole process is much simpler than you've been taught to believe.

You might begin to get a little suspicious right about here. On the one hand, I hope you've learned by now to trust the advice and testimony I've been giving you. Some of the secrets I've let you in on have made sense to you. You've tried the exercises and found that they work. You've started regaining your enthusiastic attitude.

Then, all of a sudden, I tell you how simple something is that seems to give everybody else a lot of grief. I tell you how easy a task is even though you're aware of the many complicated books on the subject. You have a right to know why people who haven't read this book find the preparation of a resume to be so intimidating.

Many people are frightened by the prospect of preparing a resume because our American educational system has sadly neglected writing ability. If that's what bothers you, don't worry about it. Writing ability is less important in resume preparation than you might expect. Somehow, many of us get the idea that a resume needs to be a great literary masterpiece, but that impression is incorrect. Remember that the simpler it is, the better it is. I can understand your reluctance to do a complex piece of writing. But I'll bet a simple piece of writing won't bother you at all. It wouldn't bother all those other people, either, if they knew the truth. The problem is, nobody ever told them to keep it simple, and they generate lots of distress for themselves by trying to create a more profound resume than is absolutely necessary.

You're not trying to win a Pulitzer Prize with your resume; you're only trying to get interviews. There's no need for fancy writing on your resume. That could very well be counterproductive to getting a job, in fact; the fancier it is, the worse it is. Keep it simple!

Here's a good rule of thumb that almost forces you to keep your resume simple: try to keep it to one page. Never under any circumstances use more than two pages.

Always use plain white 8½-by-11-inch bond paper, the kind that's in every office, the kind used in photocopying machines. Don't use fancy, ornate, or unusual type. And never use a handwritten resume. Always have it typed.

Type it yourself if you own a typewriter. If you don't own a typewriter, borrow one from a friend or family member. If that doesn't work, see if a friend can get permission to type it at his or her place of employment. And if you don't know anybody who can type and you absolutely can't get access to a typewriter, hire someone. Look in the Yellow Pages under "Typing Service." A typical price in downtown Chicago is five dollars per page, and you can usually get it while you wait. If you can't afford that, check with your local high school or library. In Chicago, for example, there are coin-operated electric typewriters at the public library downtown that you can use for a quarter, just like a video game.

Use the same fast, simple, inexpensive techniques to get your resume photocopied. If you don't know somebody who can get permission to use the copying machine at work for a personal project, copy your own at your public library. The only caution about making photocopies on a very public and well-used machine is to be sure the glass plate is clean and the contrast is properly adjusted so as to give you *neat* copies. If you can afford a little more, there are plenty of professional instant printing companies in the downtown area of any good-sized town. A typical price is about a dime per page for photocopies on plain paper for runs of one hundred copies and up.

We reviewed all those options at great length to prove a point: there's *always* a way to accomplish anything we talk about in this book. And it doesn't have to be expensive or complicated. You can "gild the lily" by making every tool you use in your job search fancier and more expensive. If you have the time, money, and inclination to go further than I tell you to go, I don't intend to dissuade you. But the purpose of this book is to show you the *minimum* efforts you have to put forth to get a good job. And the minimum is easy, fast, and cheap.

ACCOUNTING FOR PAST PROBLEMS

Before you actually start writing your resume, let's be absolutely sure that there's not another problem threatening from some dark recess of your past—another reason why you dread writing a resume.

One possible reason, one they never give you in books on how to write a resume, is that you may have something in your background that's difficult to explain in a brief, simple document like a resume. In other words, you may have a problem somewhere in your background of which you're ashamed and for which you don't know how to account when writing your resume.

If you're blessed never to have had such a problem, you can skip to the next chapter. But if dealing with that past problem is what you dread about preparing a resume, here's a way to handle those pieces of your history that need detailed, sensitive explanation.

Remember our friend George from a couple of chapters ago, the man who was a recovering alcoholic? When we met him and talked with him, when he got the chance to tell us how he conquered his problems, we became rather enthused about him, didn't we? In fact, you came to the conclusion that he was a pretty impressive guy. You felt moved to congratulate him on all the blessings he'd received and on his own attitude. You probably felt that he would be in the running if you had a job to offer.

But what if George hadn't gotten the opportunity to explain what had happened to him? What if he had simply written on his resume, "Spent 1983 in Detox Center"? We wouldn't have felt the same way, would we? In fact, George would never have gotten the opportunity to show his personality and winning attitude because he would never have gotten an interview. A human being's life is too complex and too important to be reduced to one humble sheet of paper. Your resume can't explain serious problems in your background because it can't go into the kind of detail that is needed to deal with those problems. Yet, you can't just leave a blank space, or a "gap" as we call it, for the period in your life during which you had that problem. That's what George did, and it wasn't very effective, was it?

So here's another secret: the easy way to handle such things on your resume. Do *not* write down the problem; a few words written on paper will not do it justice. Do *not* leave the time period blank; the reader will think you have something to hide, and you won't get the interview.

Instead, here's what you do. Simply write "To be discussed at interview" for any time period during which you feel you should give a personal, face-to-face explanation of your activities.

The statement lets you avoid identifying a negative on a document that doesn't allow you to tell how you've turned that negative into a positive. You won't avoid the subject forever, of course, nor do you want to. You'll tell your story at your interview, which is the appropriate place.

Writing the statement I've suggested will not cause you to lose many interviews, certainly not to the extent that identifying your past problem without the chance to explain it will. It can only improve your chances, and it will not offend me as an interviewer or turn me off to your candidacy.

Let me be clear that you're not lying and you're not hiding anything. You're merely assuring that important matters in your life get reviewed in the proper forum, not on your simple, standardized, generic resume.

You don't have to have a problem as serious as George's to be self-conscious about it. Maybe you were out of the job market for ten years because you were a homemaker during that period. Being a homemaker is certainly a noble calling. In fact, it's one that provides lots of practical experience in managing a budget, controlling your time, and so forth. These can be turned into very strong positives indeed during an interview. But you wouldn't be able to write down all those valuable experiences on your resume. And the simple statement "I was a homemaker" might make you uncomfortable, although I as an interviewer find no fault with a period of your life spent in this fine profession. But if it makes *you* nervous, use the "To be discussed at interview" statement.

Another example is a man I met while conducting a search for a banking executive. He'd always loved painting and had majored in art in college before taking up business in graduate school. After a long period in banking, he assessed his life. He discovered that he'd never scratched his itch to be an artist. The children were grown, the house was almost paid off, and he calculated that he had savings enough to last for two years, provided that he was very frugal. With his wife's agreement, he decided to quit his job at the bank and try to paint full-time.

Well, for those two years he worked very hard at trying to become an artist. He "took his best shot," as they say. It turned out to be more difficult than he thought, and when the two years were over, he found himself nearly broke and concluded that being a famous artist was not what God was calling him to after all. Naturally, he decided to go back to the banking business.

The banking business is generally (and accurately) reputed to be one that prefers very conservative employees. Any executive who wrote on his resume that he'd left the business to try to become an artist would be highly suspect. So he wrote that the period from 1981 to 1983 would be "discussed at the interview."

When he talked about how satisfied he felt that he'd at least tried to accomplish his goal, he gave me the impression that he was a very determined, mature individual. He made me understand that he'd not done something silly or "flaky" but had satisfied a deep urge of long standing. His attitude made it clear that he'd bring that same dedication back to the banking business with him and would be an even more effective employee for having resolved the gnawing uncertainty that he'd followed the wrong career. He'd turned a negative factor (an employment gap that would have been unacceptable in this particular industry) into a strong positive (perseverance to accomplish his goals even under financial risk). The opportunity to make lemonade out of his lemon came about because he didn't call attention in his resume to something that needed detailed, face-to-face explanation.

All the above cases are examples of the legitimate use of a technique to help deal with elements of your history that you fear might make you unattractive to an interviewer. Of course, if you don't have a need for the statement, so much the better. And it should go without saying that you can only use the statement *once* in your resume. If the number of delicate issues or problems in your background is such that you can't prepare a resume without repeated use of such a technique, I continue to assure you that you can still get a good job. But you'll need professional, one-on-one assistance. The solution to your job search, in this case, is beyond the scope of my book.

CHAPTER 8

All You Need to Know about Writing a Resume

= ◊ =

The organization of material to be included in your resume is really quite straightforward. There are only three essential categories of information: your personal data, your employment history, and your educational history.

A lot of resume books suggest that you include other categories as well. But I find those to be optional at best and sometimes distracting. Other categories of information don't hurt your resume, but they don't add much except length, either. The importance of sticking to the three main categories becomes clear when we look at whether including additional material adds any value to your resume.

For example, many resumes begin with a statement of the applicant's "objective." Clearly, your objective is to get a job doing something you know how to do (or can learn to do), no matter how delicately you try to phrase it. Don't limit your opportunities by implying that you're willing to consider only certain jobs. You need to talk to me about any good job I might have.

Here's another insider tip: most interviewers ignore that remark anyway. The flowery language most resume books suggest you use for your objective statement is so artificial that all those statements begin to look alike after a while; they seem empty of real content.

KEEP IT BASIC

Sometimes the inclusion of additional sections can be harmful. I remember an applicant, for instance, who had the right education and employment background for a very important job. His resume included a section on his hobbies, something many resume books tell you to include to show how well rounded you are. One of his hobbies was golf. The ability to play golf can be socially helpful to members of the executive class. But listing it as a hobby attaches more importance to it than it may really have in one's life. Had this applicant met my client, he might have impressed him favorably with his many fine qualities. But they never got the chance to meet because my client rejected him after seeing his resume. "Playing any sport well takes practice, and that takes time," he said. "If this man is so good that he tells me his hobby is golf, he must spend a lot of time on the course. This is not a forty-hour-a-week job."

You might argue that my client overreacted, and you might be right. Nonetheless, he's the CEO of a Fortune 1000 company, and the person I had to recruit was to be his understudy, the person who would replace him eventually. Overreaction or not, do you think that applicant would like to take back his reference to golf?

Here's the concept to keep in mind: the more you put on your resume, the more you give somebody a chance to object to your candidacy. Let's learn another secret at this point. Let's consider what an interviewer *really* wants to learn about you at the resume-reading stage of a search. Does he want to know about your personality? your appearance and presentation of yourself? your sales approach? your attitude toward his industry? your sense of humor? Of course not! Whether or not those things are important to the job, they don't come through well on your resume. What the interviewer really wants to know is whether you have the basic qualifications the job requires. If it's a job requiring a special degree or license, he needs to know you have it to avoid wasting both his time and yours. If it's a job requiring a minimum typing speed, he'll test you before he gives you a job; but why waste time testing someone who doesn't type at all? If it's a job where steady attendance is important, he needs to know whether you live fifty miles away or next door. If it's a job that requires previous experience, he needs to know that this is not your first job. On the other hand, if it's an entry-level job, he needs to know you don't have twenty years of experience that would make your salary expectations unrealistic from his viewpoint.

Always adopt the interviewer's viewpoint. When you do, you'll see that he only wants and needs enough information to justify inviting you to interview. And that comes from our three sections of personal data, employment history, and educational history.

Having said all that, I have to give you one exception. A section on professional involvement is appropriate if you're in the kind of occupation where credentialism is a factor. That is, if you're a member of a professional society (ABA, AAS, Million Dollar Round Table, etc.) or if you have professional publications or lectures to your credit, it is necessary to list them in a separate section(s).

WHAT TO INCLUDE

For most of us, the three basic sections are all that's needed. The time to bring up any points other than the basic facts is during the interview. We'll have more to say about such things in the chapters on interviews. For at least your first pass at your resume, stick to the three basic categories:

personal profile, employment history, and educational history.

Personal Data

Personal profile information is easy enough: that's your name, address, and telephone number. It does not include your height or weight or age or condition of health or marital status or race or color of hair and eyes. Just your name, address, and phone number. This information is usually centered at the top of the resume, as if it were a letterhead.

Employment History

Under employment history, list the name of each company for which you've worked and the dates you worked there. Do not include your supervisor's name or your references or the company's history or even its address: just name and dates. List your most recent job first. Describe *briefly* your duties on each job. During your interview, the interviewer will ask you to expand on what you've written and you'll get the opportunity to tell your story. But don't be long-winded in the resume.

If you achieved any special accomplishments on any of those jobs, list them. If you were the interviewer and your applicant had won an incentive award under his last employer's suggestion program, you'd like to know about that, wouldn't you?

Actually, what you *don't* write down in this section is as important as what you *do* write down. You know those spaces on employment applications that say "Reason for leaving last job"? People usually write "To seek better opportunity." I've seen that phrase so many thousands of times that I now assume it's the reason everybody leaves a job. If you've had five jobs in your life and you left them all "to seek better opportunity," why bother to tell me that on your resume five times? You also risk planting the seed in my mind that you might easily leave the job I'm trying to fill so you can again "seek better opportunity."

But suppose you didn't always leave under your own steam? Suppose you were what personnel people refer to as "unilaterally terminated" (what we plain folks call "fired")? Certainly there was some explanation for why you were fired, and you can give me that explanation in your interview. But it would take too long for you to explain it in writing, wouldn't it? So don't even bother to try. We'll get to it when we sit down to talk and when you have the opportunity to turn that negative into a positive.

How about writing down your salary on those jobs? Nope. The resume is not the right place for that, either. "But," you may say, "the ad to which I'm responding specifically requested my salary history."

Okay, we'll provide it. But not in the resume. You see, your resume is a generic document; you want to be able to send a copy of it to every employer with whom you seek an interview, and you don't want to have to retype it every time. Not all employers want to know your salary history or salary requirements immediately. They might want to talk to you a little bit first before getting to that subject. You certainly don't want to have different kinds of resumes for different ads, do you?

You'll respond to a request for your salary history. But not in your resume, and not in your interview, either. You'll respond through your cover letter, a document even shorter and simpler than your resume.

Never include references on your resume. Have a separate

sheet of paper with the names, addresses, and telephone numbers of your references and past supervisors. This is a good place to record your salary history, too.

I usually recommend during my job seminars that this information be jotted down on a three-by-five-inch card because most people are comfortable with that format. However, my personal preference, if you don't mind taking a little more time to do it, is to type a separate reference sheet on the same machine you used for your resume and photocopy it a few times. That way it'll be neat enough to present to the interviewer if he asks for any of the detail it contains. But either way, it will serve as a great memory aid if you're asked to complete an employment application. Your resume, you'll recall, has only the most general information. If you're asked to fill out an application, the blank may require the addresses of your past employers, and you don't want to ask for a phone book to look them up. Between your resume and your reference data sheet, you can answer any factual question you're likely to encounter on any application blank.

It begins to sound as if organizing the employment history section of a resume is pretty straightforward, doesn't it? You don't have to disclose negative facts, if any, about your employment history. You don't have to go back and figure out your salary history for every job you've ever had. All you have to do is tell where you've worked, when, and what you did there. If there's a gap, you can fill it in temporarily by writing "To be discussed at interview." And if you have any special accomplishments, you can display them to your benefit. Easier than you thought, right?

But is it equally easy for everybody? I'm frequently told that the homemaker returning to the job market after a period during which she concentrated on her family is at a disadvantage in composing a resume because she doesn't know how to account for those years. What's wrong with including in your employment history an entry identifying your profession as "homemaker" and the period during which you practiced that profession? Many returning homemakers feel vulnerable and self-conscious about writing that on their resumes. Don't be. Remember: just like all other job seekers, you only need to get an interview through your resume. If your education and experience are close to fitting the need, you'll be called. And getting that invitation to interview is all you should expect your resume to do for you. You don't need to hide your experience as a homemaker.

You're never trying to lie or hide anything when you prepare the simplest kind of resume. Nor are you trying to duck the issue or manipulate anybody. You're merely recognizing that a person's life and experiences are more valuable than the paper on which they're written.

You are too important a person to try to reduce your history and your meaning to a single sheet of paper. Let's be sure your experiences get the respect they deserve by discussing them in a proper face-to-face environment: the interview.

Educational History

The third section of information always gets shortchanged. The educational history part of your resume will probably come out rather short if you're like most people—unless you do it the way I'm going to tell you about, the way we interviewers would prefer that you do it.

It's clear why the educational history section is usually so short. Most people think of their educational experience as only the traditional formal education they've had: high school or college. Most of us can list the high school we attended; some can list a college; a few can even list graduate school;

and that's about it. I don't even want to see the courses you took or the grades you got, because I can ask you to get me a transcript if I really want that information.

It doesn't sound like very much, does it? Many of us will have only one line, and even the highly educated will have only three.

But let's think about the educational history section more broadly. And let me tell you what I as an interviewer want to see in that section. I want to know about *any* education you've had, traditional or not.

Suppose you're a data-entry operator. You must have had some training. Maybe you went to one of the computer schools. Maybe a computer manufacturer came to your company and taught you. If you've been a data-entry operator since the old days when you were called a keypunch operator, you probably had keypunch training.

If you were in the military services, you may have had some of the most outstanding training available at any price. Perhaps you went to OCS or NCO school. You may not think it has much to do with the job you're after, but I assure you that I want to know about it; it shows that someone has recognized your leadership potential and has taken steps to nurture it. That's a wonderful positive to tell me about. If you were in the Corps of Engineers, you probably have a half page of special courses you attended.

If you're a salesperson, I'll bet you've been through dozens of sales training programs. And how about all those "seminars" that only go on for a day or two but that are really specialized training?

As an example of what I call "overlooked education," let me tell you about a man at the garage where I have my car serviced. Like many other people, he didn't realize how much education he'd had until we talked about it.

New management had taken over the garage, and Lou didn't get along well at all under the new boss who had been brought in over him. It was clear that he very badly wanted to get a new job, but he seemed afraid to try. One day, I asked him why he didn't look for another job if he was so unhappy.

"I'm just a mechanic," Lou said. "Who would want to hire somebody like me? I've only worked in this one place my whole life. I guess I'd better just stay on here."

"Now wait a minute," I said. "You keep my car in top condition. You're really good. How can you possibly say you're 'just' a mechanic? That's a very good occupation."

"Don't get me wrong," he said. "I really enjoy my work. The problem is that I don't have any education at all. You see, you don't need an education to work with your hands, and all I ever wanted to be was a good mechanic. So I never even finished high school. Now it's coming back to haunt me. I don't know how to look for a new job. I could never get one, anyway, not without any education at all to my credit."

The mental phantom he'd invented for himself was so strong, I had to think for a minute to know where to start. "How did you get to be such a good mechanic?" I finally asked.

"It's all those programs I've gone through. Most of them are really good."

"Programs? What programs?"

"Well, you know, there are the ones over at De Vry Tech that they sent me to. And the General Motors ones. I really like those, because the GM guy comes right here to the shop and spends a couple of days with us. You can really learn from those programs if you apply yourself."

I didn't know much about how mechanics learn their trade, I have to admit. "Do you get any certificates from those programs?" I asked him.

"Oh, sure. I always keep them for sentimental value. Here, look."

He opened up his big red tool chest and took out a thick folder. Inside were dozens of diplomas and certificates showing that he'd received training in transmissions, brakes, tune-ups, and on and on.

No education? Why, the man had the equivalent of a college degree there in his tool chest! And it proved that he had a significant capacity for learning. But he'd always thought education meant only college credit courses. Nothing could be further from the truth.

As an interviewer, I want to know about any course or seminar that might show me not only what you know, but also how competent you are at learning new things. Tell me about it! It might be that the educational history section of your resume turns out to be as big as the employment history.

STUDY THE SAMPLES

There's little more to be said about your resume; that's how truly simple a document it is. The best way to learn to compose a resume is to read some good ones—good *simple* ones. At the end of this chapter, I've included some resumes from my files that I think make good models. Naturally, I've fictionalized all the names, but I've kept as close as I could to the original content and format. Please notice that there is no particular format that is preferred above others. Concern over format has given hours of needless headaches to job seekers. The most important thing to remember about form is what I've already told you: make it neat, and keep it short and simple. The content of your resume is more important than the form.

I've chosen a good mix of backgrounds: a young salesperson, a secretary, a service operative with a voluminous job history, and a factory worker. Also, because of their special situations, I've included a sample of a homemaker returning to the job market as well as a recent high-school graduate looking for his first full-time job.

As you read the samples, you should develop the idea that your resume is a less important determinant of your success than you've been taught to believe and that it's not to be feared. As you read them, bear in mind that they're designed only to get interviews for their writers, and judge whether they do that. Pretend you had a job to offer; wouldn't you consider inviting those people to interview? even though their resumes are all "bare bones" models? even though they are all organized pretty much along the same lines? even though they are all so simple and brief? Of course you would.

And that's the whole point of this chapter: no matter who you are, keep your resume honest, straightforward, and simple. If something doesn't add to the likelihood that you will be invited to interview, don't include it.

Don't make a copy of one of these samples, substitute your own specifics, and get it typed; that's not what they're for. In fact, copying them can be extremely risky. For example, you should notice that the resume for the returning homemaker has a humorous feeling, something you should avoid. In this particular case, the writer made good use of a natural and easy sense of humor that I later found out was one of her dominant personality traits. I included her resume to emphasize the fact that the rules of resume preparation allow for considerably more flexibility than most people think.

But notice also that the resume of the recent high-school graduate doesn't limit his opportunity by listing too many specifics. It lets me know that as a youngster just starting out, he's open to suggestions. I'd like to meet him, wouldn't you?

That's the whole idea; if I met the young man and interviewed him for a job that turned out to be a poor fit, so what? At least we had the chance to meet, and I could keep him in mind for a position that was a better match-up. And in his particular case, that's exactly what happened.

Following these examples slavishly and mechanically, then, will not be rewarding. Rather, let the preparation of your resume be another exercise for you. Don't reproduce it until you've rewritten it at least twice. Even though the resume is a simple document, there's nothing that will turn an interviewer off more quickly than grammatical mistakes or spelling errors. Remember, we have to look at the things all day; give us a break by making your resume readable, okay? Get family or friends to help you proofread it. It may take you a while to be sure your resume is free of errors, but it's time well spent.

Review your resume every day until you find a job. This not only keeps all the details of your history fresh in your mind, but it also gives you the chance to recall pertinent facts you may have overlooked before or to reword some part of it. If you've composed, typed, and copied your resume as inexpensively as I've suggested, it shouldn't be too big a chore to add a couple of lines, retype it, and run off a few copies. Maybe you won't have to revise your resume at all. But reading it daily gives you the option to do so if the need arises.

And that's all you need—really *need*—to know about resume preparation. The essentials of it are easy, aren't they? It's the fine tuning required by all the resume books that's tough. And most of us don't need that fine tuning. So don't bother with it unless you have to for some reason.

FOLLOWING UP

The other mechanical aspects of job hunting are just as simple. Take the "thank-you" note, a title I prefer to the "follow-up" note; it helps me remember that being polite is my only objective when I write one. Many job-hunting books tell you to add some additional information in your thank-you note to help "sell" yourself.

But here's the truth about following up: either the interview was successful and rewarding for *both* you and the interviewer, or it wasn't. The fanciest, most literate, most profound follow-up note in the world can't change that.

So use the rules of everyday common courtesy when acknowledging your gratitude for the interviewer's time; anything more is pointless and obvious. After every interview, send a simple, cordial note to the interviewer. It could be something along these lines:

> Dear Mr. Smith:
>
> It was a pleasure meeting you yesterday. Thanks for the opportunity.
>
> My interest in working for your company remains strong. I look forward to good news from you at your earliest convenience.
>
> > Sincerely,

Simple and polite. That's all there is to it. And it can be handwritten on personal-size stationery. All you really have to remember to do is to keep the interviewer's card so you can spell his name correctly. The thank-you note is not a sales gimmick; it's ordinary politeness. Don't try to make it more than that.

THE COVER LETTER

Another piece of paper on which job hunters spend outrageous amounts of time is the introductory, or "cover," letter.

A really good cover letter, well written and precise, is necessary if you're sending your resume as part of a "campaign" to a company that didn't ask for it. In other words, *you* are initiating the contact, and you have to let the company know why your resume is showing up in the mailbox.

A campaign is a fine way to find an executive-level job. I recommend it highly if that's the type of job you're seeking. But a campaign is time consuming, it's difficult to conduct properly, and it can be expensive. To do a campaign well, you are generally well advised to solicit professional help. Most jobs, however—almost all of them, you'll be happy to hear—can be obtained much more simply: by responding to ads in the newspaper.

If you're sending your resume in response to an ad, why do you need a cover letter at all? No matter how fancy the language over which you labor, all your cover letter can really say in such a case is "Here's my resume," which is self-evident. Consequently, a cover letter for responding to an ad in the newspaper is just another piece of paper for us busy interviewers to keep track of. So, in general, don't send one with your resume when responding to an ad; I promise you we interviewers won't be offended.

But if it's necessary to communicate one of those pieces of particular information that does not appear on your generic resume, a brief, simple, cover letter typed on 8½-by-11-inch white stationery is appropriate. The most common example is when the ad to which you are responding specifically asks for your salary history or salary requirements. Remember, that's the kind of specific data you omitted from your generic resume so that your resume can be widely distributed.

In such a case, write a simple cover letter. Something along the following lines is all that's *essential* (although, as always, you may say more if you feel it's appropriate):

Dear Sir or Madam:

The enclosed resume is in response to your advertisement seeking a widget engineer in the May 26 *Chicago Sunday Tribune*.

My most recent salary was $26,000. My salary requirement at this time is flexible.

Sincerely,

An exception to my preference for brevity involves those few cases where one of your "dream jobs" is available and your resume doesn't really qualify you. In that case, go ahead and write a cover letter, and let it sell you. That is, make sure the letter tells how earnestly you want that *particular* job. Pour out your heart, and make it the best piece of writing you've ever done.

My nephew Bill found himself in this situation a couple of years ago. He's loved baseball intensely his whole life. He tried out for the team in college but was cut early. The coach liked his determination, though, and asked Bill to be travel coordinator, moving the team to other schools for "away" games. Bill regretted not playing, but he chose to help out in the way he could, knowing that "they also serve who only stand and wait."

After he graduated, Bill got a job in the mail room of a New York ad agency and seemed to be on his way up. Then he saw the ad in the *Wall Street Journal:* a well-known sports equipment manufacturer (you see their trademark on some of the equipment at major league games) was looking for a salesperson. His dream job! It was also the dream job of dozens of mature, experienced, professional salespeople with whom Bill would have to compete.

You know, being a personnel executive has its drawbacks. All your friends and relatives think you can guarantee success in getting them *any* job. Naturally, Bill turned to me for help. It looked pretty bleak: his closest association with big league baseball was that he had driven his college team around in the school bus.

This was one of the times that a good cover letter was justified. Bill wrote and rewrote and re-rewrote his letter until his enthusiasm, confidence, determination, sincerity, and cheerfulness at the prospect of that *particular* job fairly leaped off the page. I had to admit it was one of the most direct and yet one of the most heartfelt letters I'd ever seen. I was secretly sad that this unqualified, untrained, inexperienced youngster had put so much effort into a letter that I was certain he'd send off and never hear about again.

First, I prayed for a miracle for Bill. Then I became more "realistic." I prayed that the Lord would comfort him during the long weeks that would pass with no answer until Bill ultimately gave up hope. I knew there was no way he'd qualify to represent the company to the major leagues.

Well, I was partially right. Bill's only selling to the *minor* leagues for that company today. But then again, he's still very young. Who knows what else the future holds for a worker with such a great attitude?

THE PROCESS

Here are some questions to ask yourself and answer honestly. Are you impeded in your job search because you can't seem to get started on your resume? because you can't get your cover letter composed to your satisfaction? because you're puzzled about how best to follow up? If the answer to any of these questions is yes, there's a good chance that you're doing something wrong: you're letting your resume become more important than your *self*. I can't stress enough that the job-hunting materials that are simplest to prepare are the ones that are the most effective in getting you a job. Nonetheless, it's surprising how strongly some people resist the idea that the tools and techniques of job hunting should be kept simple. In fact, you might be wondering at this point whether you should go further than the bare bones approach I've recommended.

I'll acknowledge once again that resumes and the other documents that are the subject of this chapter can be prepared with varying degrees of effort and expense; you can spend as much time, money, and energy on them as you see fit. But after my years of firsthand experience, I firmly believe that most job seekers will have excellent results with the approach I've outlined, because most personnel people require only a simple statement of historical facts to decide whether to invite you for an interview.

Compose your resume yourself, type it or have it typed, and reproduce it on a good quality photocopying machine. In most cases, these steps are just as simple as I've represented them to be and are adequate to ensure a steady stream of interviews. Also keep your thank-you notes simple, brief, and polite. Type a cover letter only when you are absolutely required to do so because the ad asks for information not included in your generic resume or because you sincerely need to call attention to some particular ability you might bring to the job.

The next step up from this basic approach is to buy a how-to book, study it thoroughly and judiciously, disregarding any advice in it that doesn't pertain to your situation, and then do a very studious job of composition. Your resume may be more formal if you do this, but it won't necessarily accomplish your objective. Your objective is *not* to have a fancy resume but to generate interviews. However, you may feel that using one of these books and contributing the time and effort they demand will help your confidence. If that's the case, go ahead and buy one; I'm in favor of anything that helps your attitude.

A print shop can typeset your resume and print it on offset equipment. This adds nothing to the content of your resume, of course, but gives it a very professional look. If you can afford this service (about one hundred dollars and up for one hundred copies on fine paper), you might want to consider it. I'm not sure it will get you more interviews, but I know it can't hurt.

Another secret you should know, however, is that personnel people photocopy the resume you submit so that it can be passed on to others having influence over the hiring decision; chances are, the manager or department head won't ever get to see the high-quality paper the printer used. Accordingly, the decision to typeset and print your resume is made more by your pocketbook than by your head.

The highest level of help is the "career service" or "resume service." The people in the resume service will help you compose your resume, have it typeset and professionally printed, and mail it out for you, often with cover letters that they help you write as part of a campaign. Such assistance tends to be very expensive and often produces a resume that is identifiable as having been written by a service. This is contrary to the image most job seekers want to convey.

Such professional help costs as much as $1,000 and can be as high as one firm I know of in Chicago that charges $3,500. Of course, for that price they provide a psychologist, give you aptitude tests, and provide "counseling." I have no wish to denigrate the many sincere, professional people in this business. I know several of them; I'm sure they do no harm and often do much good. It's just that, for most of us, such a service is considerably more than we really need. Furthermore, there's no reason to believe that the *results* are any better than those that come from a sincere, conscientious effort of your own.

JOHN J. CARROLL
1234 5th Street
Oakbrook Terrace, IL 60667
(312) 555-2286

EMPLOYMENT HISTORY:

Alpha-tech, Inc.   Oakbrook, IL
Sales Representative   5/81 to Present

- Represent state-of-the art line of modems to over 400 retailers in six-state territory.
- Provide software support for dealer network.
- Developed product technical newsletter that increased market penetration by over 15%.
- Increased territory sales by nearly 100% in just over three years.
- Increased number of retailers carrying line from 300 to 400 in same period.
- 'Rep-of-the-Month' Award, 10/83 and 4/84.

Beta Business Machines, Inc.   Oakbrook, IL
Sales Representative   7/79 to 5/81

- Sold forms and peripheral supplies to commercial customers in Chicago–West region.
- Exceeded sales quota of dollar volume each quarter.
- Exceeded sales quota of new customers each quarter.
- Quota fulfillment documentation will be furnished during interview.

EDUCATION:

- University of Chicago,   1/83 to Present
  Graduate School of Business
  (Estimated completion date: 1987)
- Illinois Institute of Technology   9/76 to 6/79
  BSEE   6/79
  - XEROX Sales Training Program   4/82
  - BBM, Inc. Sales Institute (NYC)   9/79
  - In-house sales and technical courses
  and seminars at Alpha-tech   5/81 to Present

MARY LOU CARROLL
123 East 6th Street
Chicago, IL 60660
(312) 555-1234

EXPERIENCE

Downtown National Bank and Trust Company.
(March 1979 to Present Time)
Secretary, Commercial Loan Department.
- —Perform all secretarial functions for three commercial loan officers.
- —Type correspondence, memos, loan documents, and statistical typing.
- —Assist customers of bank on telephone and in person in absence of officers.
- —Coordinate quarterly presentation of portfolio status report for Office of President.

South Side Trucking Company.
(June 1978 to March 1979)
Secretary and General Office.
- —Performed all secretarial functions for small, inter-city trucking company.
- —Typed invoices, bills-of-lading, and correspondence.

EDUCATION

Senn High School	September 1975–June 1978
Commercial Course	
Typing: 70 wpm	
Shorthand: 90 wpm	
Roosevelt Business School	April 1980
Word Processing Course	
(NBI, Wang)	
American Bankers Association	
"Introduction to Computers"	May 1981
"Spreadsheets"	October 1982
"Using Databases"	November 1983

AFFILIATIONS

American Secretaries Association
American Bankers Association

William P. Carroll, Jr.
1234 W. 7th Street
Evanston, IL 60055
tel. 312/555-9876

I. Work History

A. From November 1982 to March 1985. Stockman at Chicago Shoe Company. Responsible for keeping stock in order. Also responsible for taking semi-annual inventory.

B. From August 1976 to September 1982. Security guard at North Side National Bank.

C. From January 1976 to August 1976. Assistant baker at National Bakeries, Inc.

D. From July 1971 to December 1975. Counterman at McDonald's.

E. From June 1967 to June 1971. U.S. Army. Honorable Discharge June 1971. Rank: Master Sergeant.

II. Education

A. Walker Technical High School, Chicago, IL. September 1963 to June 1967. Graduated.

B. Clerk's School, 1968 (U.S. Army)

C. NCO School, 1968 (U.S. Army)

D. NATO Coordination, London, 1969 (U.S. Army)

E. Hamburger University, 1971 (McDonald's)

F. Security Classes, 1976 to 1982 (North Side National)

G. CPR and First Aid, 1979 (North Side National)

H. Crisis Management Seminar, 1980 (North Side National)

JAMES JOSEPH CARROLL

1234 8th Street
Chicago, IL 60601

312/555-5678

Work Background

Chicago Casting Company
(9/81–5/85)

CHIEF MACHINIST. Responsible for prime-shift operation of Suncutter AOM-3 five-axis machining center, including fixture design, set-up of piece-part, and monitoring of machine cycles. Work includes finishing of investment castings and contouring.

Responsible for determining tooling needs and for ordering tooling in advance of production run.

Special accomplishments include coordinating installation of new "third-generation" control unit.

Midwest Machining Company, Inc.
(4/78–9/81)

MACHINIST. Responsible for third-shift operation of Cincinnati Milacron Drill-Matic 4. Work involved drilling aluminum to MIL-SPECS for civil aircraft industry.

Riverside Tool Works
(1/72–4/78)

APPRENTICE. Served apprenticeship on variety of milling machines and drill presses: Cincinnati, Suncutter, Parsons, DMG, etc.

Work was primarily of a job-shop nature.

Educational Background

Suncutter Corp.	AOM-3 training.	1/82 thru 4/82.
IIT	Parts programming training.	8/82.
Riverside Tool	Apprenticeship.	1/72 thru 4/78.

CLARETTA JEAN CARROLL
321 Ninth Street
Lawnwest, IL 60011

312/555-9912

Employment

1962 to Present Time: Homemaker.

> Responsible for all aspects of operating busy sub-urban home.
> Complete responsibility for budgeting.
> Skilled in communication and conflict resolution.
> Developed word-processing skills (Wordstar system, 80 wpm) and spreadsheet skills (Lotus system) on personal computer.

1959–1962: Bookkeeper (Full-charge).
Abacus & Sons, Inc.

> Set up and administered manual bookkeeping system through general ledger for mail-order firm.
> Supervised two other bookkeepers.
> Left position to raise my family.

Education

1955–1959. Woodrow Wilson Commercial High School.
Received diploma 1959.

1965–Present. West Suburban College. Both credit and noncredit courses through W.S.C.'s "Continuing Education Program." Courses included: Accounting Review, Introduction to Computers, and Bookkeeping Computer Systems. Transcript can be furnished during interview on request.

A. MARK CARROLL
1234 8th Street
Chicago, IL 60601

312/555-5678

EDUCATION:

Wentworth High School. September 1982–
June 1986.
Graduated June 1986.
Grade Point Average: 2.8/4.0
Track team, three years.

Wentworth Junior College (Evening Division).
Enrolled for 6 credit hours (business).
Classes begin September 1986.

EMPLOYMENT:

Joey's Finer Foods: October 1984 through present.
Perform wide range of retail-related
tasks as assigned by store management.
Earned 100% of my educational expenses and spending money.

North Shore Assembly Church: March 1985
through present.
"Junior Group" Assistant (Sunday
school).

CHAPTER 9

How to Win as a Newcomer to the Job Market

$$= \Diamond =$$

While the simple steps to job-hunting success that you've read so far apply equally well to all job seekers, many of the examples have been about people who, for one reason or another, have lost their jobs. But what about the person who's never had a job to lose? Is the first-time job seeker different in some way from others in the job market? Does that individual have problems that deserve special mention?

I've had ample opportunity to observe new entrants to the job market, particularly younger ones, at firsthand. My work occasionally takes me to colleges to participate in on-campus recruiting at the request of my clients. The idea behind these "Career Weeks," as they're usually called, is to bring representatives of many companies to the campus all at the same time so that those about to graduate can meet potential employers and schedule job interviews as efficiently as possible.

Every time I've participated in such an event, I've been impressed anew with how frightening it is to be looking for a job for the very first time. College or high-school graduate, teenager or middle-ager, male or female, all have that same taut look of fear on their faces. That includes even those with stellar academic records who you'd think would ooze confidence.

It's true that there are special problems associated with being a first-time job seeker. But they're problems that also provide *special opportunities* for someone who comes afresh to the job market with a good attitude.

Let's start our examination of those opportunities by admitting candidly that the reason for the first-time job seeker's fear is a very good reason indeed: his own recognition that practical experience is one of the most important assets a person can bring to a new job. That's an undeniable fact; it's obvious that employers should and do prize experience highly.

But if the new job seeker limits his understanding of what constitutes value in an employee only to practical work experience, naturally he'll be afraid of the prospect of looking for a job. He'll be frustrated by his lack of work experience, and this will make him insensitive to his real worth to a potential employer.

Read that last paragraph again carefully, because it contains the seed of a wonderful opportunity for the new entrant to the job market: although work experience is an important asset, it is not the *only* asset that pays big dividends when looking for a job. Not all work experience is of good quality, and some counts for very little to an employer. I recently interviewed an accountant who claimed long practical experience. But as the interview progressed, I saw that he hadn't kept up with the latest accounting practices, hadn't *developed* in his career. Does such a worker have twenty years' experience, or one year of experience twenty times?

The experience that others bring to the job market should never frighten you as a competitor for jobs. You have an asset, a special value, that evens things up. To help you understand and believe your value as a new entrant to the job market, think for a moment about this: companies retain people like me and pay our high travel expenses in order to recruit *inexperienced* people. Doesn't it seem reasonable that there must be something special, something important, about first-time job seekers that would justify such expense and effort? Doesn't it seem that there must be some unique value associated with a new worker?

We recruiters know exactly what that value is, but most first-time job seekers don't, which means it's time to share another secret of the recruiting business with you. It has to do with the "trainability" of the new entrant to the job market.

You see, companies in today's complex, high-powered economy change constantly. Procedures and goals sometimes change on a daily basis in some industries. One of my clients likes to say that nothing is constant in his company except change. In such an environment, the most desirable employees are the adaptable, flexible people. In other words, the employees most in demand are those who can demonstrate an ability to *learn*.

If you've just come onto the job market from school, whether college, high school, or trade school, and whether you're a graduate or not, who is in a better position to demonstrate an ability to learn? Surely, the experience of learning new things must be very fresh for you. Recognize that wonderful capacity in yourself and take joy from it; it helps you draw even with the older, more experienced worker who may no longer be as quick on the uptake as you are.

The next time you hear the remark "There's no substitute for experience," you can agree with it cheerfully rather than dread it. You can also thank the Lord for your understanding of the special kind of experience you're going to bring to your new employment, not work experience but learning experience. It's a form of experience that you can and should mention explicitly and confidently to any interviewer.

Regrettably, that kind of experience isn't especially meaningful when printed in black and white on your resume; it's certainly not as easy to deal with in written form as direct, on-job work experience is. It would seem that the first-time job seeker would have only a lot of white space in the employment history section of his resume. But if you've had summer jobs or part-time jobs after school, list them. This advice is applicable only to newcomers to the job market. I urge more senior job seekers to list only full-time jobs because most part-time jobs held as a student have little relevance to the kind of full-time work being sought. But identifying part-time jobs will display the first-time job seeker's sense of responsibility, will show that he has good work habits, and will much improve the presentability of his resume.

Some personnel counselors instead advise the recent entrant to the job market to compensate for his lack of job experience by describing the kind of job he'd like to have. But that's a perilous suggestion. What if you describe the job you'd like but the people you're talking to don't happen to have one of those? You might eliminate yourself from consideration by a very good company that way.

Your learning experience means to me as an interviewer that your mind is fresh and that you're *able* to learn. The next question about which you must reassure me is whether you're *willing* to learn. And the only way to display that willingness is the same way you'll show me everything else that's good and desirable and important about you: through your attitude.

> ● **Rule 14 is that employers find the first-time job seeker's freshness and adaptability as attractive as the veteran's practical experience; make sure you let them know you're ready, willing, and able to work hard for your start.**

Showing that you're ready, willing, and able to work hard displays the other assets you have that will appeal to a prospective employer: the energy, the *enthusiasm* that others feel are the hallmarks of youth but that we have seen to be a natural and logical result of the Christian attitude. Your determination to do a good job is an asset that you possess in abundance even if you're an older job seeker such as a mother who is returning to employment outside the home after raising her family or a senior citizen who has found that retirement leaves too much idle time.

RE-ENTERING THE JOB MARKET

Returning to the job market after a long absence can be every bit as scary as looking for your first job. But your principal job-hunting asset remains unchanged throughout your entire life: your positive attitude. As a re-entrant to the job market, you can proceed with the same zest and vitality as does the new entrant; you're on an equal footing.

Yet, the returning homemaker squanders opportunities by displaying the opposite characteristics, by coming to the market haltingly, almost embarrassed to be asking for an interview. It's something I'll never get used to: who could possibly be embarrassed by having taken time off to raise a family? Is there any human activity more important, more noble, more worthy of our applause? Then why do you, as a returning homemaker, act as if you've been doing nothing but loafing for the past few years? You've been one of the busiest workers in the world!

Your family has been your firm. You may have been in charge of the accounting and bookkeeping departments. You've been responsible for transportation, communication, and administration. You've run the cafeteria as well as the switchboard and message center. You've been everything but the plant security force, and maybe even a little of that. As a result of such a wide range of experiences, you bring to the job market maturity, levelheadedness, and that all-important intangible, "seasoning."

What you can do that nobody else can do as well is cope. It's something you've had to learn in order to survive in the tough world of making a home. Don't be ashamed of it. One thing you really know how to do is work!

There's no need to be shy about the wisdom your maturity has instilled. Your particular blessings are much in demand if you have the right attitude. For example, let me tell you briefly about a piece of original research conducted and published by my firm (*Profile of an Executive Secretary,* 1985, Interviewing Dynamics, Inc.).

This research resulted from a survey in which hundreds of Chicago-area top secretaries and their bosses were polled on what makes a good secretary. In each case, the secretary who participated in our survey was the highest-paid secretary in the company. I think you'll agree that this was a pretty select group.

Among the many other findings too numerous to detail here, we found that senior executives prefer secretaries in their forties or fifties. The executives cited such virtues as "stability" when defending that preference. Here are some of the comments that the executives wrote about their important assistants: "well organized," "serious," "I don't have to worry about who's keeping an eye on things when I'm away," and "She knows how to make do."

And of those secretaries over forty, *87 percent had taken time off* (defined as being at least five years) *to raise their families.*

So don't ever be embarrassed about coming back onto the labor force after managing your home. You're just getting to the age when you're at your best, and the business world knows it and is eager to hire you. Be confident and happy about it.

In other words, there's nothing that sets you any lower than your younger rivals. You have every bit as much energy and enthusiasm as they have, and as you know, they're what get you a job.

But let me warn you of a danger: that natural energy and enthusiasm can become a drawback if it's channeled in the wrong directions. Take the case of my nephew Jeffrey, for example. (That's right, another relative story. There's nothing like being a personnel executive to help your family stay in touch!)

Jeffrey had been looking for work for months with no success at all. Beyond a vague feeling that "Interviewers don't like me," he was unable to suggest any reason for his lack of results. He finally decided that it wasn't his fault. He concluded, "Nobody will hire me because I don't have any experience; but how can I get experience if nobody will hire me?"

There's nothing particularly original about that quotation, of course. I've probably heard it even more often than you've said it if you're young and unemployed. But it's another of those myths that have been invented to make being out of work less unacceptable to you than it should be. The fact is that nobody could have a second job unless he'd had a first job; it's just common sense that everybody had to start somewhere, and you can find your start, too. So if you're young and claim you can't find any work at all, try some other explanation, because the one that nobody will give you a chance just doesn't hold water.

My brother asked me to sit down with Jeffrey and find out

what was really wrong, so I scheduled a mock interview for him at my office. At first, all went smoothly. Jeffrey is a likable and presentable young man with interest in the communications field: advertising, publishing, broadcasting, public relations. He has completed one year of college and is continuing in night school.

The kind of job he wants is one where he can learn, he told me, and this aspect of his attitude is to his credit. He told me he was willing to start as a page or delivery person or whatever was needed if only he could learn the business from the ground up.

This kind of talk made me very impressed with Jeffrey as a candidate—until I asked him what salary level he had in mind.

"Six figures," he said without hesitation.

When he saw my expression, he hastily added, "Oh, not right away, of course. I mean after I learn the business; say— about two years from now."

Jeffrey was throwing away one of the greatest blessings of the youthful job seeker: because they're typically just beginning to accept financial burdens, the young are usually in a position to work a little bit *cheaper* so that they can get their first break. It's something that every company's personnel interviewers know and consider. It's a consideration that can be criticized as crass and discriminatory, but there's one way in which it's very fair—it compensates the employer for all that training he's going to have to give you in order to capitalize on your fresh learning ability, which is why he hired you in the first place.

It's also a pattern that applicants themselves appear to recognize and accept; some recent original research performed by my company showed that salary is not the main goal for new entrants to the job market. Rather, they list as their top priorities the chance to use a variety of skills (so they can find out what they really enjoy doing) and the opportunities for promotion in the future. Salary was a distant third.

Here's another secret of the personnel business, one that people who advise you to interview aggressively always seem to overlook. Personnel interviewers are *not* the most highly paid employees in a typical corporation. Salary studies my company has performed show that most of them (about 67 percent) earn between $19,000 and $24,000 a year. That's a very attractive salary level, well above the norm. But it may give you some idea why aggressive salary demands are not likely to win a newcomer any friends in the personnel department.

At the time I interviewed Jeffrey, I didn't know the source of all the propaganda that had confused his mind. But I probably could have figured it out if I'd taken the time. It seems he'd been reading those contemporary books that offer advice on gaining advantage over others through such unacceptable means as psychological aggression and verbal intimidation. He'd also talked to a guidance counselor at his school who told him to demand a salary at least several times what he thought he was really worth and to "control" the interview aggressively; I suppose the guidance counselor had been reading some of those same books.

This "pop power" movement has created a sense today among young people in business that it's right to be competitive to the point of combativeness. Consequently, it may be fashionable to be assertive. It might even make you feel good to display your dominance. But it probably won't help you get a job. Humility is more attractive in a first-time job seeker than is the modern competitive spirit. Understand that humility does not imply inferiority or subservience. Humility means an accurate, unbiased, sincere assessment of one's worth and dignity, such that instead of humility, we could simply use the phrase "being realistic." Few personal characteristics better indicate a correct, attractive attitude than proper humility. It is a characteristic so important that we are reminded by Proverb 15:33 that "before honor is humility."

So please be careful of those books that instruct you to act arrogantly. The behavior patterns they teach are sometimes contrary to a Christian way of life. If you're young and looking for your first job and if you want something to read, try the want ads.

And just so you don't think I'm nagging you, I'll tell you in the next chapter the *special* way to read the want ads that assures as many interviews as you can handle—even if you're a "rookie."

CHAPTER 10

How to Find Out Where the Jobs Are

= ◊ =

Many of the how-to-get-a-job books today concentrate on the "mail campaign" approach to soliciting interviews. This is probably because of that inside tip I gave you earlier: the very best jobs often are not advertised. The mail campaign is an excellent way to get at those jobs in the hidden job market. In fact, it is second in importance only to networking through friends, family, and business associates.

But the strength of the mail campaign and of networking leads some authors to virtually ignore the Help Wanted newspaper ad—the source of the *greatest number* of jobs available. Don't put the cart before the horse. Your chances of finding a good job quickly from a newspaper ad are far, far better than finding the same job just as quickly by any other means.

Therefore, let's do something a little unusual, something most of the how-to books disregard. Let's learn how to examine the newspaper effectively for jobs.

USING THE BEST SOURCE OF JOBS

Most people turn to the classified ad section to find job information. That's the right thing to do, because most of the Help Wanted ads will be found in this section. But notice that I said *most* of the ads. That definitely does not mean *all* of them. You ignore other sections of the newspaper at your peril when you're looking for a job.

The business section of the *Chicago Sunday Tribune* has more pages of Help Wanted ads than it has of business news; these are full-time, high-paying jobs, often the best ones in the paper. The home section sometimes advertises for people to do part-time work from their homes. And the sports section also has part-time job offers, particularly during times such as play-off season when extra help may be needed.

Sections other than the classified and business sections are unlikely to offer many jobs that are either full-time or permanent. But a part-time job is often a godsend for somebody who's been out of work for a long time. Part-time or temporary work might also be perfect for the homemaker who wants to ease back into the discipline of the job market. And you might get to see a free baseball game as well! So don't ignore *any* section of the paper.

The Sunday paper is usually the happiest hunting ground for the job seeker, of course. Page after page of glorious Help Wanted ads. More than you could possibly contact. So many, in fact, that their very quantity causes you to make your first mistake. You go to that part of the alphabetical listings where you expect to find your perfect job. If you're a secretary, you look under *S;* if you're an engineer, you look under *E*. Finish that letter and you're through, right?

Wrong!

The only right way to read the classifieds is to start at the very first ad under *A* and go through the very last ad under *Z* with a pen in your hand to circle the many, many offers to which you'll want to respond. Here's why: ads are usually classified by the person at the newspaper who takes the ad over the telephone. And very frequently that ad taker doesn't pick the same word you or I would pick to alphabetize.

Let's say you're looking for a job as an accounting clerk. Look under *A*, of course, for "accounting." Then look under *C* for "clerical." But please don't forget *B* for "bookkeeping." And then there's *F* for "financial." If the job is with an insurance company, it might be under *I* for "insurance." The same job at a brokerage firm might be under *S* for "stocks and bonds." If the job involves using a computerized accounting system, you might find it under *D* for "data processing." If it's offered by the Zappo Company, it might even be under *Z* for "Zappo."

Get the idea? You have to go through *every* ad. I know that's a lot of reading. But it's only because there's a lot of opportunity for you.

Because there are so many ads, when is the best time to go through them? Monday morning, bright and early, when you're fresh, right?

No! That's the worst thing you can do. Let Saturday be your big day for job-hunting effort.

Most Sunday newspapers come out on Saturday; in Chicago they're out by early afternoon. Be at your local newsstand waiting for the truck to deliver those papers. Take Saturday afternoon and evening to go through the paper in great detail, identifying your opportunities.

Use two different colored pens. Use one color to circle those ads that list a phone number to call, and use the other color for those ads that ask you to send a resume. It will be a long task, but it will be worth it.

Identifying your opportunities is only part of your task; you need to do two more things on Saturday. First, address envelopes for all those ads that asked for your resume. Put your resume inside, seal and stamp it neatly, and take them all out to a mailbox as soon as you're finished. Get them into a mailbox as soon as you can; there may be a mail pickup in the evening. Get those resumes on their way to your future success.

GETTING YOURSELF READY

The second thing you need to do is to get ready for an interview on Monday. You don't have any interviews lined up yet, but lay out the clothes you would wear anyway. Why? You *might* have an interview Monday, even though all you've done so far is study the paper and mail your resumes. You'll see shortly how that can happen.

Be sure your suit or dress is pressed. Pick a clean shirt or blouse, and make sure it has all its buttons. Don't wait until you're getting dressed for that interview you might have to find out that there's a button missing or a zipper that won't close. Shine your shoes. They don't have to gleam like patent leather, but they must be cleaned and buffed.

Lay out all that stuff you put in your pockets or purse: your wallet, your keys, *two* pens (in case one dries up while you're trying to fill in an application), change for public transportation and phone calls, and whatever else you customarily carry around with you. Then make sure you have a neatly folded copy of your resume and your reference data sheet or three-by-five card in the pocket of whatever you've picked out to wear. Also, if you need someone to watch your children, make sure you know when that helper is available.

The object is to be as prepared as a fireman is to get going on a moment's notice. And this is an exercise you'll repeat every night before you go to bed until you get a job. To see if you're doing it right, ask yourself whether you'd be ready to go in fifteen minutes if somebody should call and offer you a good job. That's how prepared you have to be.

You'll probably be exhausted by the time you tumble into bed Saturday night. Good. That's a sign that you're doing it right. You'll be refreshed on Sunday.

Sunday is the most enlivening day of the week, the Lord's Day. Enjoy your personal relationship with Him at church, and give thanks for the opportunities He's in the process of giving you. I'm sure that's advice you expect from me by now. But there's another personal relationship that will invigorate you on Sunday as well, and this is a good time to remind you of it.

Enjoy your family; forget about your unemployment woes, because they're almost gone.

In many ways the most fiendish aspect of unemployment is the way it leads you to neglect your family and your friends, the way it makes you turn inward to wallow in a private problem. But you don't have to submit to that kind of solitary misery anymore; your unemployment problem is going to go away soon enough. The beginning of the end of your unemployment woes will be tomorrow morning. So rest with confidence after your delightfully refreshing Sunday; get a good night's sleep. But set your alarm clock for 7:00 A.M.

> ● **Rule 15 is to live your life as if you're working, even when you're not. Start by getting up at your usual hour or even earlier. Stay clean and well groomed. In other words, *respect yourself*.**

No rolling over for another forty winks on Monday morning. Out of bed and into the shower. Brush your teeth, comb your hair, shave—look, just be ready to *go*, okay?

CALLING FOR INTERVIEWS

By eight o'clock, be next to your phone. Have the following tools by your side: the newspaper you marked up Saturday night with places to be called, a writing pad, a pen, and a copy of your resume.

But don't pick up the phone just yet. First, list your negatives and scratch them out with vigor. Then, list your positives and count your blessings. Review your resume once more in case anybody asks you for some fact about your history. Now you're almost ready to begin.

Some people get a little nervous at this point. You can see it coming, can't you? You're going to have to pick up that phone and *call somebody*.

It may help you to know that everybody is affected the same way. At my company, when we run an ad listing a phone number, we sometimes get more resumes in the mail than we get phone calls. Don't *you* make that mistake; don't be afraid to use the phone. The telephone is one of your best friends when you're looking for a job; there is no faster way to line up interviews. The postal system is a boon as well, but it's second in importance to your phone. By the time your mailed resume reaches me, the job may have been filled by somebody who called me about it.

If I give you a phone number in an ad, I want you to use it. As you'll see soon, calling the interviewer is not only the fastest way to an interview for you, but it's also the best way for the interviewer to get quick action on the job he's trying to fill; it's best for both of us. So please don't be tense or shy about calling; if we give you a phone number, we *want* you to use it.

My industrial training friend recommends taking a few slow, deep breaths before you make that first phone call. That works pretty well. But if you want *my* prescription, repeat the following verse ten times slowly and meaningfully and out loud. It's from Psalm 7:10, and it never fails to remind me that I shouldn't be afraid: "My defense is of God, / Who saves the upright in heart."

Now you're ready to start placing your calls. Here's your objective: to get two interviews a day until you get a job. No more than two. One in the morning and one in the afternoon. Please keep that objective in mind: you're trying to get interviews. Your objective is not to get a *job* as a result of these phone calls. If that's what you hope to get, you'll be disappointed. Companies don't hire people over the phone. I don't want you to be disappointed, and neither do you. We want your attitude to be a shining, smiling one based on realistic expectations. So don't expect a job offer until you've had the interviews. If you can get two interviews a day, I guarantee— flatly *guarantee*—that you'll have a job offer in far less time than you ever thought possible.

Let me add immediately that I'm asking you to do another of those insider things: call the ads early on Monday morning. You will not get this advice from the how-to books we talked about before. In fact, you will get the opposite advice; you'll be told *not* to call on Monday morning. This is a trap—a well-intentioned trap, but a trap nonetheless. The people who write those books tell you what they sincerely think all of our personnel colleagues want. And the common misconception is that our colleagues want to be left alone on Monday, so they can plan the rest of their week and so forth. This is nonsense.

The old saw The early bird gets the worm applies to job hunting as well as to so many other things in life. In fact, I've compiled a statistic that demonstrates it. At my company, more than 70 percent of our clerical and entry-level jobs are filled eventually by applicants who called the first day the ad appeared. That's nearly three-quarters of the jobs we offer, and yet the myth persists that you should never phone personnel people on Monday.

A friend of mine recently wrote an article for one of the Sunday supplements in which she gave the usual advice about Monday morning calls. She went further; she repeated the conventional wisdom that resumes should be mailed near the end of the week so that they don't get lost in the "crush" that comes in right after the ad runs. She's not only my friend, she works for me. I called her into my office as soon as I finished reading the article.

"Remember that ad a few weeks ago where your phone number was misprinted?" I asked. The paper had printed the number with only six digits. Nobody could possibly figure out how to call about the ad.

She grimaced and said, "Don't remind me. It was awful. I just sat around all day. I was sure glad the newspaper fixed it in the next edition."

"Uh-huh. And you wanted to be called, didn't you? You wanted to be called beginning first thing Monday morning."

"Well, of course. How else could I do my job?"

"Yet you wrote this article in which you advise people not to call about ads on a Monday."

"Oh, that. Well, that doesn't mean *me*. But a lot of other personnel people don't want to be contacted early on Monday. Everybody knows that. I wanted to tell applicants not to alienate the interviewers by bothering them."

"So, where did you get that opinion? From some of our consultants here?"

She looked blank for a few seconds. "Well, no, not from any of our people. But I'm sure that's the way it is. It's one of those things everybody just knows."

"Maybe our competitors feel that way?" I asked.

"No, of course not. Our competitors are all on the ball. It's as you always say, 'Thank the Lord for our competitors because they keep us on our toes.' No, I can't think of any of our competitors who are reluctant to get phone calls on Mondays."

"Okay, Joyce. You know everybody in town who's in our business. Name me any two personnel people who feel that way."

She thought about it for a while and wasn't able to come up with even one name, which didn't surprise me a bit. The fact is that personnel people want you to call about their ads. In fact, they *need* you to do that if they're to continue being personnel people. One of the ways personnel people are rated by *their* bosses is on how well their ads "pull"; that is, by how successful they are at arranging interviews with qualified candidates.

Don't wait until Tuesday to call ads that appear in Sunday's paper; the job may be filled. Call Monday. In fact, try to be among the first callers. Try to be "firstest with the mostest."

And don't be nervous. Remember that the interviewer needs for you to call. You're doing him a *favor* by calling as soon as possible.

It's time to remind you yet again of the secret that attitude gets hired before skills. The time to begin showing that shining attitude of joy and confidence is during your first phone call. Be happy. Be assured. Be confident. And why not? After all, you're doing everything exactly the way the interviewer wants you to do it so far, aren't you?

Now here's another secret for you. You can *hear* a smile. No, really, you can. I've received tens of thousands of phone calls from applicants during my career, and I promise you it's true. An experienced interviewer can hear that smile in a caller's voice. There's something in the tone of a smiling voice that I can't explain to you in words. But that smile comes to me over the wires as surely as if I were seeing the caller.

I feel good about somebody who smiles, don't you? Everybody does. Put that big smile on your face when you call; I assure you the interviewer will hear it. It's a good preliminary indication of the kind of attitude you have.

Tell the interviewer you were attracted to his ad and that you're available for an interview appointment at *his* convenience. He'll probably have some questions for you before he invites you to interview, questions that ask you to tell him a little factual information about your experience. He probably *won't* ask at this point about your strengths and weaknesses or your likes and dislikes. He probably *will* ask about such things as whether you're presently employed, where you last worked, what your job was there, and when you left.

Some applicants might hem and haw at this point, unsure of details like that. But your smile will stay confidently in place. It might even get bigger because you've got your history written down on your resume right in front of you. You can tell the interviewer what you've been doing and where and when. Furthermore, you can do this very quickly and precisely because you've kept your resume short and simple, and you reviewed it only a few minutes earlier. It's beside you, and you can summarize any part of it that the interviewer asks about. Very quickly, you'll be able to be even more helpful by offering him a choice of interview appointments and asking which would be convenient for him. Ask something along the lines of, "Is it convenient for you to see me this afternoon, or would tomorrow be better?"

Try to put yourself in the interviewer's place. First thing in the week, you're called by a bright, shiny, smiling applicant. The caller sounds so "up" that you like him right away; talking to somebody who's cheerful and helpful is a great way to start the week, isn't it? When you ask the applicant to tell you a little about himself, he gives you a concise, precise summary of his job experience, all in that same happy, smiling tone you heard when you first picked up the phone. He's even showed his cooperative nature by suggesting he can come in when it's convenient for you and suggesting a couple of alternative times for getting together.

You know what you'd do if you were that interviewer? You'd check your calendar to see if you could meet the caller today. You'd really want to meet the guy! He sounds like he has a terrific attitude, doesn't he?

Here's a fact: people will not only want to hire you if you show your pleasant, positive attitude; they will *like* you better.

Should it happen that the interviewer finds it convenient to see you right away, be ready to go! Out of your jeans and into your interviewing uniform. Unless, of course, your jeans just happen to *be* your interviewing uniform.

CHAPTER 11

The Rules of Personal Appearance

= ◊ =

Time now to address the important subject of your general appearance for an interview. Many of the how-to-find-a-job books deal with your appearance and with dressing for success. It's a fact that appearance is important in business; this gives many of these books definite value to the business-person. Some of the people who are knowledgeable in this field are friends of mine, and I can assure you that they really understand the implications of clothing choice, color choice, and so forth. If you're already moving quickly up the corporate ladder, these concerns may help you get to the next rung a little faster. But if you're not on the ladder at all yet, you may have concerns of a more basic nature.

As was the case with the resume books, the authors of "how-to-dress-for-business" books are speaking to an audience that doesn't include some of us, at least not yet. I don't want you to have the impression that only an expensive, dark blue, three-piece wool suit with a costly white shirt and silk tie will get you a job. If you already have "corporate clothes," by all means wear them on interviews. But if you're out of work, you may need your money for other things. You can't afford to let your shining attitude grow tarnished by baseless worries about the quality of your clothing.

Actually, dressing too well can be counterproductive for some interviews. Looking like you just stepped out of the pages of *Vogue* or *Gentlemen's Quarterly* might give the interviewer the impression that you're a fashion plate who's not prepared to work very hard.

I'm going to tell you the truth again, truth based on actual experience, not theory: clothes are only one aspect of your total appearance. There are other aspects of your total presentation of yourself that are as important as (and sometimes more important than) your clothing choice. You may need to work on them as well.

Paradoxically, clothing is the easiest aspect of your appearance to deal with. So let's talk about clothes first, and get that concern out of the way.

Here's another inside tip for you: not every interview will be improved if you wear a suit. There are jobs characterized as blue-collar jobs that are very lucrative and for which a suit is inappropriate. Believe it or not, it is perfectly all right to wear jeans or similar attire for such an interview. Wearing a suit for interviews in many blue-collar occupations will actually lessen your chances of getting the job. So if you're applying for a job as a trucker, a punch press operator, or a dockman, go right ahead and wear your jeans if that's the appropriate attire for that line of work.

However, those clothes must be clean and neat, as must be your shoes, your fingernails and, indeed, every part of you. It's not clothes that make the man, in this case; it's the neatness of those clothes.

For *all* other types of jobs, for all white-collar, office, executive, sales, or professional jobs, business attire is mandatory. You may not like to wear a suit. You may resist wearing a tie if you're a man or heels if you're a woman. You certainly have

139

the right to make such choices. But if you do, you're not likely to get any of the office or professional jobs I'm offering; it's that simple. Take your choice.

A suit is best for both men and women. Don't rush out and spend your rent money on a new suit, though. The same rules apply to the suit wearer as to the jeans wearer: make sure what you wear is neat and clean. The more conservative your suit is, the better it is for interviewing. But cleanliness is more important than conservatism, if there's a choice between the two.

A white shirt or blouse is better than a colored one. Dark shoes are better than light ones, and black ones are best of all. And so on and so on. You can spend much time and money figuring out how best to dress for business. But if you're unemployed, you may have neither enough time nor enough money to deal with such issues.

The point I'm trying to make is that the degree to which you develop your business-appearance style depends on your pocketbook. If you have enough money, by all means follow the rules laid out in the many excellent books on how to augment your chance for success through attire. But if you're broke, don't give up hope. Go with "neat and clean" and you'll be even with the guy with the five-hundred-dollar suit, because your best raiment is your closely woven, well-tailored attitude. Come to think of it, that might even put you *ahead* of the guy with the five-hundred-dollar suit!

There's another aspect of appearance that's a little harder to deal with. It's what I call "grooming," for lack of a better term, although it includes more than is usually implied by the word. By grooming, I mean any personal habit or adornment that might make you look different, noticeably different, from the current American norm. It includes hair, fingernails, beards, and so forth, things that people regard as very personal, that are a part of them, and that they are reluctant to change. And sometimes that reluctance to change personal grooming habits is all that stands in the way of landing a new job. Let me tell you about a man I'll call Phil who interviewed with me for an accountant's position.

Phil was in his early forties and had good experience and education. His work record was quite attractive. But when I presented him to the people who made the final decision, he was turned down flat after only the briefest of visits. I sat him down and tried to give him some idea of what his problem was.

"Phil, you might find success is easier to come by without those sideburns," I said.

He looked startled. "What sideburns?"

What sideburns indeed! They were more than sideburns; they were the old style known as "muttonchops." They stuck out more than an inch from his cheeks. They were unkempt, frizzy, and very prominent. "*Your* sideburns," I said, pointing at them.

He felt his jowls and looked surprised, as if he were aware of them for the first time. "Do you think they're too much?" he asked.

Too much? He looked like he had a couple of brown golf balls hanging from his ears!

As we talked, I began to realize what had happened. Phil's whiskers had grown over a long period, starting out when he was a teenager. Long sideburns were in style then, and he probably thought he looked like Elvis Presley. That may have been true then, and it may have been important to him at the time. But lots of years had passed. Today he looks more like Elvis than he does like, say, Linda Evans, but that's as far as the similarity goes.

Over the years, Phil's sideburns had grown more and more

extreme until they were the only thing one noticed about him. But it was gradual. He saw himself in the mirror every day, and the change never really dawned on him until I pointed it out. Phil got rid of those bulging side whiskers and very quickly found a job. He'd limited his horizons in order to preserve something that really wasn't all that important anyway.

That's why you have to take a very careful and a very honest inventory of your appearance and why that inventory has to examine more than just your clothes. Hair that is too long, unkempt, or outrageously coifed or colored is a barrier to employment. Likewise long or dirty fingernails, gloppy jewelry, heavy perfume or after-shave, sunglasses worn indoors, and all those other things that may start out reasonably but grow to ridiculous extremes over time. Don't feel too bad if some fashion of the past or some peculiar current fad has gotten out of hand with you; as it is truly said, All fashion ends in excess.

But please do something about your fashion excesses before they get in the way of landing a job. And don't give me that tired old story about how Jesus had long hair. Jesus let His appearance correspond to the norm for the time and place when He was on earth. I ask you to do no more than that. Make your appearance as much like the current American business norm as you can. Modeling your daytime business appearance after the modern American norm does not destroy your individuality; it lets your *real* individuality—your personality, your attitude—get noticed.

And here's a promise: anything you cut off will grow back. Just get rid of it, please, for the interview. Younger people in particular sometimes resist this advice. But if you want a job, you have to follow the rules.

● **Rule 16 is that you don't make the rules. The employer does. Follow the commonly accepted business appearance rules, at least until you get your job.**

This chapter is deliberately short to characterize the kind of importance my experience has taught me to attach to the subject. I cannot emphasize strongly enough that neatness, cleanliness, and adherence to the norm are the critical aspects of your business appearance. As your pocketbook begins to bulge, you can go on to fine-tune your business wardrobe. But if you ever show up at my office for an interview, I'll expect you to be neat and clean.

CHAPTER 12

Networking and More

= ◇ =

Up until now, I've been encouraging you to perform all your job-hunting chores by yourself. I continue to feel that's the fastest, cheapest, and best way to find a job. But even though you now have the confidence to charge ahead on your own to land that terrific job, I have to admit that it sounds kind of lonesome. Even though you may not need it, strictly speaking, it sure would be nice to have a little help, wouldn't it?

Lots of people are willing to help you. Some will help you out of friendship and love, others out of a sense of duty and obligation. Still others will help you because they can make a profit doing so. But as far as your job search is concerned, it doesn't really matter why they want to help, only that help of all kinds can be had.

One thing is certain: although help is available, you won't get it unless you *ask* for it. That seems obvious, but I want to be explicit about it. When people are facing difficult situations, they often think less clearly than when things are going well. Many people in such situations will begin to feel that all they have is their "self-respect" and that admitting they need help is harmful to that self-respect. The young person overwhelmed by fear of rejection when he looks for his first job may feel this way. The homemaker, coming out after twenty years at home, may feel that asking for help is a poor way to begin facing her younger competition. The unemployed production worker who's been looking for six months and doesn't know where to turn because his industry doesn't seem to want him anymore may want to preserve his "pride."

But you can't afford such self-indulgence. The worst thing you can do is to scorn the help of all those who want to make your path smoother. Let me show you what I mean.

THE STRANGE CASE OF WALTER

Some time ago, when I was first starting my trading company, my brother asked me to schedule some time to talk to a friend of his. (Relax. This is *not* another story about one of my relatives.) I naturally assumed that the friend (let's call him Walter) was looking for a job and wanted some advice. It was a hectic time in my life, and frankly, I tried to convince my brother that one of my consultants could do just as well.

"Oh, no," my brother said. "He was very insistent that he speak with you personally. Nobody else will do, he said. He said he knows of your reputation."

Well! Who wouldn't be flattered? I set an appointment for that afternoon and spent the morning looking forward to meeting my "fan."

When Walter arrived, he looked all around my office, which is filled with a lot of mementos. He stared at a plaque on my wall and asked what it was. That's pretty typical behavior for a bright applicant, and you can learn a lot from it: always try to put the interviewer at ease. Let it be your responsibility to make that kind of "small talk" that puts people at ease on first meeting if you sense it's needed. I told him briefly the story of how I got the plaque for a speech I delivered in England some time ago. It's a good story and used up about three minutes. He sat on the sofa, beaming. I figured the ice was broken.

When I finished, I leaned back. "Well, Walter, how can I help you?" I asked.

He made some remark about the view from my office. As I said, many people start with this kind of banter, and I accommodated him by pointing out a few landmarks. Then I asked again what I could do for him.

He told me what a good friend he was of my brother, how they'd frequently played golf together, and how things were going in their suburb.

After a few minutes, I again asked what he wanted. My smile was beginning to look a bit forced, I'm afraid.

He started to talk about the lobby in our building and how he enjoyed the art deco restoration.

"Wait a minute," I said. "You didn't come to see me to admire the lobby or look out my window."

He looked uncomfortable. "I—I wanted to meet you, get to know you," he said.

"Look," I said, "I don't want to be rude, but I'm trying to get a new business off the ground and I really have to—"

He started beaming again. "Oh? What kind of business?"

Nobody likes to talk about her business more than I do, so we spent another ten minutes discussing the problems of international trade. But I still had no idea what he wanted.

I guess he saw me looking at the Wrigley Building clock out of the corner of my eye, because he suddenly looked at his watch, jumped up as if he'd forgotten an appointment, thanked me warmly for my time, and left. I never saw him again. I immediately called my brother and asked what this peculiar visit had been about.

"Beats me," he said. "He never said exactly why he wanted to meet you. He just asked me to arrange an introduction. But I'll call him tonight and find out."

He found out, all right. Walter told him I was the best "contact" he'd made so far. It was only after probing to find out what kind of contact Walter seemed to think I was that the truth emerged. Walter had lost his executive job with an insurance company—a whole year earlier! It was the first my brother had heard of it. In fact, it was the first anyone in their neighborhood had heard of it. Walter had continued to get dressed every morning as he always had and to head into the city at the same time as always, discussing the *Wall Street Journal* with his fellow passengers on the train. But he never mentioned his unemployed status to anyone. He probably listed all the passengers on that train as contacts. And so, perhaps, they would have been—if he'd swallowed his pride and asked for help.

That type of thing has happened to me countless times during my career, though not to that extreme. Because it's so common, we can learn a lot from Walter's story.

WHAT NETWORKING IS

Walter had started out with a very good idea. He was trying to "network." There is no more effective way to find a really good job. It is the number one technique of job hunters. Although I cannot prove it, I believe that more white-collar jobs are found by networking than by all other methods put together. I cannot say enough good things about it.

Apparently, other people espouse it as strongly as I do; it's a hot topic in the personnel field today, one that has brought about a proliferation of books and seminars on "how to network." But you might as well go to a seminar on how to breathe air; networking, for all its immense value, is the simplest, most natural thing in the world, and we all do it.

Here's all it is: letting as many people as possible know that you're looking for work. Why? Because lots of jobs are known to be available only by people who currently work in the company. The more people who know you're looking, the greater the likelihood that you'll hear about something. It's the way that a smart job hunter can make his own breaks, for as Francis Bacon noted, "A wise man makes more opportunities than he finds."

Some of us have a network ready-made, just waiting for us to use it to find a better job. If you belong to a professional association, for example, the directory of your membership is a marvelous, ready-made network. Say you're an accountant; there are both local and national organizations of which you might be a member. Who would be more likely to know about good accounting jobs than your fellow accountants?

If you don't belong to a professional association, consider joining one. *Professional* as used here is not used in the sense that refers to people with specific collegiate training, such as doctors or lawyers. Rather, it refers to your particular occupation or, sometimes, to the occupation you'd like to have. It's a sort of loose-knit club of people who are all in the same line of work.

Professional associations exist for just about any occupation you can think of. There are associations for doctors, medical assistants, and lab technicians. There are associations for senior executives, junior executives, and secretaries, for salespersons and sales trainees. There's even an association for presidents of companies. No matter what your occupation, there's a good chance that an association of your colleagues exists. Joining that association will improve your professional standing, help you grow in your career, and—not coincidentally—be a ready-made network for times when you need to look at other job possibilities. The best way to learn what associations you might want to join is to call on your local Association of Commerce and Industry (most big towns have them).

Of course, the primary purpose of professional associations is not networking; their purpose is to foster education, set standards, promote mutual marketing, and so forth. But at the same time, they just happen to serve the networking purpose well.

There are, of course, many networks designed for the specific purpose of helping their members get ahead in business. And because getting ahead frequently means taking another job, these networks are referred to simply as "networks" rather than "associations." They are composed sometimes of people in the same occupation but more often of people in different occupations who have other characteristics in common. For example, there's a network of women who work in downtown Chicago. There's another of women who work on North Michigan Avenue, there's one for women who work in retail, and so forth.

You probably have access to some terrific ready-made networks. It may be that your church has a job bank. Don't expect your pastor to come over to ask you to use it. Even if your church doesn't have an active job bank, isn't your membership roster a great ready-made network? And how about the alumni list from your college? from your high school? or both? Ready-made networks are not as effective as networks that you build yourself from the ground up, but they're a lot easier and faster.

I suspect Walter had access to plenty of ready-made networks had he chosen to use them. The insurance industry, being well established, has many associations, clubs, and societies. But the fact that he chose not to use them is not necessarily a mistake. He might have intended to build his own network. There's nothing wrong with that; it's just that Walter did it poorly.

HOW TO NETWORK

Building your own network involves letting everyone you know or meet find out that you'd consider a career change. It also involves getting to know some new people. And the more important they are, the better.

This is the part of networking that I find difficult to talk about. It seems so mercenary, so calculating for a networker to try to meet people for the express purpose of getting a boost in his career. And yet, many lifelong friendships arise from networking contacts. But it requires a boldness, which is to say a lack of that vicious pride that makes you self-conscious, to put yourself forward. Nonetheless, that's how you build a network. Here's what you have to do:

- Make sure everybody you talk to is able to discover that you'd "consider a career move" (that's the trendy way of saying you need a new job).
- Make sure you ask all the people you talk to for the name of somebody *they* know who might know of a good job. Ask to use your friend as a reference. (Ask: "May I use your name?")
- Then contact the person whose name you were given, whether through an appointment arranged for you (as was the case with Walter) or through contacting the person and requesting that appointment yourself.
- After each interview, keep in touch (follow up) with your contact on a frequent, prearranged basis. (Ask: "May I call you again?")

Suppose you start with only two contacts in your network. (That's not too tough; most of us could come up with the names of at least two people in our businesses who would be willing to talk to us about our career paths.) And suppose that you follow up every two weeks (not unreasonable). Now suppose further that everybody always supplies you with a new contact (don't count on this happening with this kind of consistency).

Obviously, this is an idealized example designed to show you the mathematics more than to be a guide for behavior. After about three months, you'll have more than one hundred contacts to put your name forward as part of your "extended personal sales force": people in your business, people who share some of your personal characteristics, people whom you come to genuinely enjoy over time, important people who might know of good jobs.

If Walter had followed that pattern for the twelve months he was unemployed, he'd have made almost thirty-four million contacts! (Okay, okay, I *said* it was an idealized example.) You see how the math works; there's no way you can fail to get a job—and make a lot of friends—if you build a network properly.

Networking properly isn't easy, however. For one thing, like everything else connected with your job search, building your own network requires that your attitude be in good shape. It means you'll have to ask your business associates, your friends, even your family, for help. You'll have to ask them to do at least part of your job search for you, the part that involves finding new contacts.

You owe it to those helping you to follow through on every source they mention; you can do that only if you're poised and self-confident. Picking up the phone and calling a total stranger in this way is foreign and frightening to most people. So you'd better take a "humble pill" before you start to put your network together.

What's the best way to contact those new people? The telephone is probably the fastest. If a secretary or receptionist stands between you and your new contact, be perfectly candid about your reason for wanting to meet the boss. Use the name of the person who referred you (remember to get permission!) to help you get through.

The letter approach to contacting new names for your network is easier but slower and (in my experience) less effective. Basically, you'll need to construct a good letter explaining your reason for writing, your background (many people enclose a resume), and a very specific request for an appointment. This last point is the one most frequently overlooked by would-be networkers, just as it was by Walter. You *must* meet people you intend to put into your network. Even if it's just a phone conversation as opposed to a face-to-face meeting, you must have personal contact to build an effective network. Sending your resume off into the wild blue yonder without a personal follow-up is an exercise in futility. It wastes paper and postage. Worst of all, it makes you unjustifiably comfortable by causing you to think you're doing something productive when you're not. The poorly conducted network or mail campaign is, in fact, another of those traps into which the unwary job seeker can easily slip.

In a sense, I'd almost rather see you do nothing than simply play at networking and mail campaigning. At least doing nothing about finding a new job forces you to be aware that you have a problem; you're not misled into complacency by thinking you're doing all you can.

If you're getting the idea that networking can be challenging because of all the discipline required to make a credible attempt at it, you're right. But don't be afraid of that challenge. You'll need to be prepared and organized. Keep notes. Record the particulars of everybody you meet, as well as the substance of every conversation you have as a result of net-working. If you get an opportunity to do a good turn for one of your contacts along the way, do it graciously and willingly. Be consistent; follow every lead that you discover. Be pleasant; thank every contact for the time spent with you. Be thought-ful; never waste the contact's time. Networking cannot be done properly without organization, preparation, and dili-gence. But given those tools and your attitude that allows you to make a stranger into a friend, you have what you need.

GETTING PROFESSIONAL HELP

Several times, I've advised you to get professional help if you have a serious job-hunting problem. This is the kind of help from your friends that turns a profit for somebody. But again, why be concerned about that so long as your special problem is being addressed?

One of those special problems, curiously enough, might be that you make a lot of money. How can that be a problem? The more you're worth on the job market, the more difficult it is to find a position. The reason is obvious: there are fewer high-paying jobs than low-paying jobs. Consequently, the higher you are on the corporate ladder, the more you need to do a good job of networking. Remember how networking operates: the number of people who can help you keeps going up. You need to get all those numbers on your side.

Therefore, it might seem that turning to professional help is a good idea. And so it is. There are many consultants who can help you do a good job of networking. Naturally, their value to the job seeker will often be reflected in their cost. But if you want to stop being the president of a Fortune 1000 company and become the president of a Fortune 500 company, the cost is probably well worth it.

My purpose in writing this book, however, is not to address the top levels of management. People who have made it that far are usually quite skilled in the art of getting hired. Those of us who have not yet had such stellar success, though, are still advised to turn to professional help. The problem is that unless you know how to judge the quality of the help offered, you might find yourself being hurt rather than helped.

The time has come, therefore, to talk about the structure of the personnel recruiting business. First of all, there are three levels: high, middle, and low. These adjectives refer not to the quality of the applicants they are intended to help, but to the quality of the counselors assigned to do the helping.

The Executive Search and Full-Service Firms

The higher-level personnel companies are often referred to collectively as the executive search firms. Their counselors generally have advanced degrees. Some of the people in our business who handle, for example, financial recruiting assignments may have a master of business administration degree behind a bachelor's degree in liberal arts and, perhaps, a master of science in personnel administration as well. Obviously, they don't recruit beginners because, as you can imagine, their time is very pricey. These firms tend to be associated with one of the large accounting or management consulting firms, although some are separate partnerships. In any event, if you've never heard of any of them and don't know what I'm talking about, that's a good sign that you're not yet in their league. If you're in upper management, you probably make it a point to have lunch with one or two directors of research every few months, so you don't need to hear anything from me other than "Keep it up!"

Many of us will encounter a different kind of "helper for

hire": the middle level or full-service personnel company. Although the consultants who work there are often well educated and well connected, they are neither to the extreme represented by the highest firms in the business. Mostly, the full-service firms recruit at high- and middle-management levels but often hire for high-paid, nonmanagement specialties (such as engineers, bankers, etc.). Frequently, they will recruit clerical employees, often to assist the professional-level workers they've recruited. They often specialize in "staffing up" an organization, recruiting some workers at the very low end of the pay scale as well as some at the upper end.

When you get a chance to meet a consultant from one of these firms, jump at it. No matter what your level, such firms have an assignment somewhere for which you might be right simply because they handle all levels.

The Employment Agency

Now we have to talk about a different type of personnel company: the employment agency. Many employment agencies are absolutely topnotch, grade A, number one, professional companies featuring a level of help equal to any a job seeker can get anywhere else in the recruiting industry. I applaud agencies that behave professionally. I have friends in that business. And I even refer people to them.

Having said all that, I still have to admit that the proportion of outstanding counselors tends to be lower in the employment agencies than it is in the executive search or full-service firms.

Mostly, employment agencies do clerical or entry-level recruiting. Accordingly, there's no need for counselors at such agencies to have any special training, so they don't. Agency counselors generally do well enough with a high-school education or less. Also, in some states, no licensing is required. Understand that I'm not trying to be arrogant here: I'm simply pointing out that you have no assurance beforehand, either through training or through state licensing, about the competency of counselors at some employment agencies. Beyond any doubt, some of them are among the most professional and dedicated people in the world. But you can't assume that with the same degree of safety you can with a consultant who works for one of the higher-level firms.

The watchword, therefore, is *caution*. Try to avoid, for example, signing anything indiscriminately if you go to an employment agency. Some agencies require you, the applicant, to pay a fee when you find a job, and the application they ask you to sign may have a clause to that effect.

But in many parts of the country, the industry standard is for all fees to be paid by the prospective employer. The regrettable (and, as far as I'm concerned, immoral) practice of collecting fees from both employer and applicant is known as "double dipping" and is more common than you might think among "body shops," particularly in states where regulation of employment agencies is nominal.

My warning about signing anything holds true even when the counselor has specified that the employer pays all fees. What he may not tell you is that there's usually a "guarantee period" during which the employer's fee is refundable should you decide to quit. And some agency applications are really contracts that obligate you, the applicant, to pay that fee in such cases. Under those circumstances, you not only wouldn't have the job anymore, but you'd wind up owing somebody money for it!

Although I can't tell you how good or how bad any counselor chosen at random from the employment agency field might be, there's one sign I can give you for sure: if a counselor asks you for money, run! If you are being pressured into signing something before you feel you've had enough time to study it to your own satisfaction, run! You may be dealing with someone who is less than ethical.

Be sure you understand that I'm not condemning all employment agencies; there are many outstanding ones; those are the ones that want the riffraff run out of their industry as much as I do. Likewise, all the other services that may provide professional assistance to you—resume services, copy services, and so forth—will and *should* charge you a fee.

Always keep in mind that your interests may not be uppermost in the mind of your counselor. His own self-interest (human nature being what it is) may intrude on his objectivity. To see how this is likely to be true, consider that he's paid only if you take a job. That's right: he probably gets no salary. If you don't take a job, he doesn't eat. Under those circumstances, he will be tempted to urge you to take a job—any job—without a lot of concern about whether it's right for you or for the employer. He may yield to the temptation to tell you that you're "overqualified" for the job you want, to tell you that "good jobs are hard to come by," and so forth. In other words, he may perpetuate some of the myths that bury the good attitude we've been working so hard to resurrect.

Again, the employment agency in your town may be above reproach; I certainly hope so. But please check with the Better Business Bureau before you get too involved with an employment agency. This is what you'd do with any company with which you were considering major dealings, isn't it? Before you buy a used car or a house, don't you check to assure yourself you're dealing with a reliable company? Should such an important decision as who will help you with your job search be handled any differently?

It is also appropriate at this point to repeat some advice I offered earlier: don't let *any* job-hunting tool or technique monopolize your time. Don't put all your eggs in one basket. Approach your job search on all fronts simultaneously. If you want to register with your local employment agency after you've taken the time to become comfortable with the people there, do so. But don't count on your agency counselor to find a job for you. The best he can do is to give it a good try; that should be enough to satisfy you because you're proceeding on your own as well. In other words, the employment agency is just one more tool in your job-hunting bag. Never rely on it exclusively.

Remember: all the things we've discussed to this point—the resume, the cover letter, and the thank-you note, the network and the employment agency, the ads in the paper and all the rest—are important *only* insofar as they help you get an interview. The interview gets you the job, and it's time to talk about interviewing.

Now the real fun begins.

CHAPTER 13

How to Prepare for Your Interviews

$= \Diamond =$

There are two kinds of preparation you have to do in order to interview well. One kind of preparation involves a little bit of research. You'll repeat this little bit of research for each of the interviews you arrange for yourself. The other kind of preparation involves knowing what questions you'll be asked and readying your answers so they come out with the kind of enthusiasm and confidence you feel inside about a new job. That preparation, which is the subject of Chapter 14, will only have to be done once, and it will take you through all the interviews you'll ever have.

Let's focus in this chapter on the kind of preparation you'll do before every interview. We've already looked at part of it: getting your "interviewing uniform" ready the night before and grooming yourself early in the morning so you're set for the day, ready for any interview opportunity the Lord might send you. Being thus physically ready is a good start, but there's more.

GOING TO THE INTERVIEW

Showing up on time is one of the best indications of the kind of attitude you'll bring to the job. Certainly you have every intention of showing up on time for every interview. But sometimes things have a way of getting out of hand and making you late; being late is an accident.

Being on time, however, is *no* accident; it shows you know how to think ahead and control events. So plan your route the night before. If you'll drive, make sure you know where you can park. If you'll be taking public transportation, find out what route to take and whether and where you need to transfer. Early on in your job search, call the transit company and request a transit map. Most big cities also have a Transit Hotline or similar service that you can call to have a route figured out for you.

Estimate the amount of time you need to get to your interview, and then add thirty minutes. This allows for missed transit connections, poor weather, and other unforeseen circumstances. It also allows for the fact that you may not be as good an estimator as you think.

But suppose you make all your connections, the roads are dry and fast, and you show up a half-hour early. Do *not* go in that much ahead of your appointment. We can find a better use for that extra time.

There's something you have to remember: the company is interviewing you, but you're also interviewing the company. You've been feeling that all the judgment will be made by the company about you. But it goes the other way, too, doesn't it? You'll be passing judgment on the company. So use the extra time to look over the area and make some judgments of your own.

How convenient is the company to public transportation? Even if you plan to drive to work, you need to consider public transportation for those times when your car is in the shop or when the weather is too bad to drive. How close is the bus stop? Is there a parking lot? How long a trip was it for you to get there, and is it realistic to try to make that trip every day?

Taking a job too far from home is almost a guarantee that your attendance will suffer, and this is a consideration to keep in mind when deciding whether to accept a job offer.

Also examine the company's premises. Do they look neat and safe or slipshod and careless? Look the neighborhood over. Is it the kind of area where you'd feel relatively safe if asked to work overtime?

About five or ten minutes ahead of time is when you should present yourself. You've already been in the area for quite a while, getting the "feel" of things, so you're in no rush. Chances are you'll give your name to a receptionist and be asked to have a seat. Relax. Remember that the company has already spent a lot of money to attract you; newspaper ads don't come free. Nor does the interviewer's time. The firm must really want *you* pretty badly. Remembering this logic ought to help ensure your calm disposition.

Most people get a little nervous before an interview. But you know what? That's perfectly all right. In fact, it's desirable. Studies have shown that performance is best when you're ever so slightly tense. So please don't let that touch of tension concern you. After all, a little bit of tension is just a sign of your excitement and enthusiasm for this job, and that's not so bad, is it?

If you're more than a little tense, however, we ought to look for a reason. Some people are just naturally shy. They worry about meeting people and about putting themselves forward. They feel they're not "good enough" for the situation and are flirting with disgrace, humiliation, and pain. I know you're not one of those. If you've gotten this far in the book, any suggestion that you're not good enough is a suggestion that I won't listen to. Your determination to find a job shows that you're a winner.

I've always thought Isaiah was very reassuring to people

who felt shy or embarrassed about themselves. In fact, he made quite an issue of it. Isaiah 50:7 says, "For the Lord GOD will help Me; / Therefore I will not be disgraced." And if *that* isn't strong enough, we read only a little later in Isaiah 54:4, "Do not fear, for you will not be ashamed; / Nor be disgraced, for you will not be put to shame."

You see, it's not *possible* for you to be humiliated. The Lord will go into that interview with you, if you invite Him. He'll be happy to accompany you, and He'll be proud of how well you've done the rest of your preparation for this company.

LEARNING ABOUT THE COMPANY

Proper preparation consists only of knowing something about the company. I'm going to give you a list later of the questions you're most likely to get from the interviewer. One of those questions will probably be answered by what you've learned about the company.

You can learn a great deal about most corporations from the public library. Many sources are available to tell you all you care to know (and more) about corporations. Rather than try to list all those, let me suggest that you ask the librarian for help.

What if the interview is to be at a small company, not a big corporation? No problem. Phone the company and ask to speak to someone who can tell you a little about the operation. If a receptionist answers, you might be asked to hold for a while until somebody who does public relations work gets on the line. But it's highly unlikely that your request will be refused. People *love* to talk about their work. Besides, you're looking only for very basic information; you just want to know what the company makes or what service it provides.

Take notes. Then see whether the company makes a product you've used or provides a service for which you've had a need.

Once you get somebody started explaining the company to you, you may be surprised at how much information will be offered. In fact, you might hear more about the company than you really need to know at this point.

There's nothing inappropriate about calling a company and asking for information of this kind. Your interest is sincere and complimentary to the company. It's unnecessary as well as immoral for you to make up some lie when asking for this information. If you're challenged about why you're asking, tell the truth. Simply state that you're scheduled to interview for a position and you'd like to find out a little more about the organization before your appointment.

There's no way this can hurt you. In fact, the person you talk to might keep your name in mind as somebody who showed a mature, sincere interest in the organization and who gave him the very pleasant opportunity to talk about what he does for a living. Let's face it: it never hurts to have a friend in the company, and a phone call like this just might make one for you.

FOUR SIGNS OF FRIENDLINESS

Actually, we can take this notion of making a friend at the company one big step further. Let's see exactly what happens when you first meet the interviewer. You've just gotten to the interviewer's office and greeted him with a big smile and a firm handshake. You memorize his name when he introduces himself and use his name when you tell him you're happy to meet him. You look him in the eye as you say this.

These four elements of greeting are so important, I want to

repeat them. In fact, you ought to memorize them. Through the years of my experience, I've been amazed at how few applicants display all four of these simple elements of cordiality. Yet I believe that these four elements used at first meeting will take you half the way to making the interviewer feel warm toward you. In fact, they're so important that I've set them aside as a rule.

> ● **Rule 17 is that there are four simple
> signs of friendliness that must be part of your
> greeting at *every* interview you ever have.
> These "friendly four" are**
> —**a glowing smile,**
> —**a firm handshake,**
> —**direct eye contact, and**
> —**correct use of the interviewer's name.**

Practice. Study your smile in the mirror. Ask friends to evaluate your handshake. The use of the masculine pronoun in this book is intended to be neuter, and so should your handshake be. That is, your handshake should be the same whether the interviewer is male or female: it's firm, neither crushing nor limp. Nothing else you can do will put the interviewer so at ease as calling him by his proper name while you shake his hand firmly and making solid eye contact while you show that sincere, open smile.

Now wait a minute here. Did I say "put the interviewer at ease"? Isn't the objective to put *you* at ease? No, you're already at ease. You know the company better at this point than anybody there knows you. You're prepared, and you've invited the Lord to sit with you during the interview. You're in the driver's seat!

Help the interviewer to be as comfortable with the process

as you know you'll be. Your smile reflecting your good attitude, your firm handshake, and your cordial greeting using the interviewer's name as you meet his eye are a good start in that direction.

You see, the interviewer may be a little nervous, and it's to your benefit to help him out. Why should he be nervous? Consider his position. He really needs to hire a good employee for this job. The department head on whose behalf he's interviewing has probably been asking him for results. He would like to hire a winner. Hiring you would make him look good.

And that's the thing to keep in mind: the interviewer *wants* to hire you. He wouldn't be spending his time and his company's money if that weren't the case.

Of course, you know how it is when you make a decision. Sometimes you're just not sure you're doing the right thing. And although the interviewer wants to hire you, he needs to reassure himself that he's making the best choice. You'll want to help him reassure himself by continuing to display that winning attitude and by answering confidently and directly any questions he may have. Having prepared in advance for those questions shows the respect you have for the company and for the interviewer's time.

It shouldn't be too difficult to predict at least some of the questions you'll get; most of us interviewers ask the same ones. They're in the next chapter.

CHAPTER 14

How to Make the Interviewer Your Friend

$$= \Diamond =$$

An interview is similar to a social visit. It's like responding to the question posed by an old friend you've not seen in a few years: "What have you been doing?" or, more commonly, "What have you been up to?" It certainly shouldn't be threatening. In fact, you ought to look forward to it as a pleasurable experience. The best interviews are those that end with both parties feeling that they've been sitting at the kitchen table chatting.

The responsibility to be sure you come away from an interview with that warm, cordial feeling doesn't rest solely with the interviewer. You share the responsibility because you're part of the interview—probably the more important part. You'll want to be careful, therefore, to do your part well. A few very basic rules of behavior will help.

So let's alter slightly the analogy of an interview as a social visit. It might be better if you thought of it as a "formal" social visit, like a graduation ceremony for a relative where you want to be on your best behavior. During the formal social visit of the interview, therefore, you'll politely decline any offer of a cup of coffee, even if the interviewer has a cup. You won't chew gum or bite your nails or suck on mints, either. In other words, let your mouth be free to answer the interviewer's questions and to ask some of your own as well.

Often the interviewer will ask questions that appear to be designed to put you on the defensive. Such questions are one of the reasons why so many people dread interviews. But, as always, try to see the interviewer's point of view and you'll understand that he's not trying to put you down.

You see, the interviewer feels a little defensive, too. He's concerned that you won't inflate his turnover figure, for example. *Turnover* is the relation between the number of employees recruited by that interviewer and the number that "didn't work out." It's one of the measures of performance that the interviewer's boss uses when rating him. That is, turnover is one measure of how well the interviewer is doing his job, and it strongly influences how much he's paid, his chances for advancement, and so forth. Doesn't it make sense that the interviewer will ask questions intended to assure himself that you're one of the candidates who will work out and who will stay with the company for a long time? The questions the interviewer will ask you are not intended to embarrass you; they're intended to protect him and his company's investment in you. And if you're going to be a member of this company, it's good to know that care is taken in such matters, isn't it?

The interviewer is not your enemy. When you accept this, your orientation toward interviewing will be more favorable for your success.

Actually, the interviewer's questions are not at all important; only your *answers* are important, and he knows that. His job would be much easier if he could just say, "Please help me to hire you by reassuring me that it's the right thing to do." The only way he can get that reassurance, though, is by asking you questions. So don't take his questions as a challenge or as an attempt to make you uncomfortable. As the saying goes, Don't take it personally.

Rather, turn the interviewer into a friend by helping him to ensure his own continuing success. Remember that the interviewer wants to hire you. But he's cautious about taking that big step. An applicant with a good attitude assists the interviewer to resolve this painful and frightening doubt.

How in the world can you help the interviewer? If you feel that he has all the power and that you're the one being judged, you can't help him. You'll be too defensive to do your part well. You have to remember that you're in the driver's seat, that you're really the one in charge of the interview. Your task is merely to avoid giving reasons *not* to hire you.

QUESTIONS TO EXPECT, AND HOW TO RESPOND

One way you can help the interview rests on your understanding that the first question you're likely to get during any interview is probably the most important one. It sets the tone for the rest of the interview. That first request is often deceptively simple: "Tell me a little about yourself."

Until you know something about the nature of the job you're there to discuss, you can't answer that question helpfully. Trying to talk about your skills and preferences before you understand the job is a waste of time. There's nothing wrong with the question; it's one of the most important questions the interviewer will ask. It's just that it always comes up too early in the interview. The typical interviewer thinks he's "breaking the ice" with that question, but he's often working in opposition to his own goals. I caution consultants in my company against beginning an interview that way.

Once you see that the request "Tell me a little about yourself" is asked at the wrong point in the conversation, the way to helping the interview along is clear. Move it to the proper time in the interview. The proper time is much, much later.

Common courtesy requires you not to ignore the question, however. So smile and tell the interviewer where your last job was and why you're attracted to his company. Use that little bit of research you did to find out what product the company makes or what service it performs. If I were interviewing at, say, a computer manufacturer, I'd answer that question by saying something like, "I live in the Old Town area in Chicago, and I was with the Downtown Bank, which is very close by, until about a month ago. I responded to your ad because we used your model 72 computer at the bank, and I heard the computer people say it was a fine product." And then, the very next thing I'd say (without giving the interviewer the chance to ask another question out of sequence) would be, "Can you tell me a little about the job?"

This is a polite and helpful response. It provides a *brief* and respectful acknowledgment of the interviewer's question. If you're not able to truthfully give any reason why the company is attractive to you because you don't yet know enough about it, say something like, "I'd like to tell you a great deal about myself and my abilities, but I can best do that if I understand the position. Can you tell me a little about the job?" Notice that you always come back to finding out about the job. And why not? Isn't that what *you're* there to learn?

Actually, interviewers recognize the need for you to have the opportunity to ask about the job. The last question they usually ask is, "Is there anything *you'd* like to ask *me* about the job?" It's regrettable that this is the *last* question they ask; it really ought to be the first. You're helping by moving that question, which must be asked and answered anyway, to its proper time in the interview. You're in the driver's seat, so steer the conversation where you know it needs to go.

A lot of job-seeking books demand that you "control" the interview, that you manipulate the interviewer. When making these suggestions, some of these books suggest that you come perilously close to lying. I'm opposed to that on moral grounds, of course. But I'm opposed to it on common-sense grounds as well. Lying is no way to start off a relationship as important as your new job, is it? Besides, attempting to manipulate the interviewer is a fruitless exercise; he's a veteran of one thousand interviews versus one for you. There's no way you can win such a battle of wits.

But helping the interview to move along smoothly and successfully is quite a different matter. It wouldn't be necessary if all interviewers were trained to conduct interviews in the same way and in the most efficient manner possible. But business schools don't teach interviewing, and most interviewers learn their craft by apprenticeship. Under such circumstances, it's necessary for you to help out all you can. Be sure you *listen,* then, when the interviewer tells you "a little about the job." You want to be able to help him understand how the work experience or the life experience you have had relates to the job that needs to be done.

By way of example, suppose the interviewer tells you the job requires customer contact. When it's your turn to talk again, you can let him know how much you enjoy meeting and working with people. Most applicants enjoy working with people, and you can let your excitement at this prospect show immediately. Or suppose the interviewer tells you that this job requires flexibility or adaptability. Isn't he really saying that this job is something new every day? And if you're anything like most applicants I've met over the years, that characteristic of the job would be extremely attractive to you.

Your positive attitude consists of both example and witness, of "show" and "tell." But "show" is more important than "tell" in a job interview. It's not enough to say "I like the challenge of working with people" or "A job where there's something different every day is exciting to me." You have to *show* your enthusiasm for such a job, your confidence that you can do it, your sincerity in wanting to do it. In other words, display your positive attitude again. Let that smile get a little wider. Let your eyes get a little brighter. Really *show* the interviewer that he has captured your interest.

Finding out more about the job before you talk about yourself also helps deal with two other typical questions that you'll get on almost every job interview: "What did you like most about your last job?" and "What did you like least about your last job?" A variation on these questions is, "What are your strengths and weaknesses?" The theory is that you like those activities in which you are strongest. But if you stayed on that last job for any significant length of time, you had the chance to find many characteristics that you liked about it. How can you know which of those fifty or one hundred characteristics are meaningful to the interviewer? You certainly don't want to talk his ear off all morning telling him every little detail of those things you found attractive about your last job. The only sensible way to handle the situation is to listen when he tells you about the job he's offering and then pick those things from your last job that he'd want to know about.

Handling the "What did you like least?" question is a little different. The problem here is that an applicant who doesn't have the right attitude fears the interview and wants to get it over quickly. As a result, such an applicant answers questions too tersely, without sufficient detail to make his meaning clear.

Let's suppose for the sake of discussion that you're tempted to say you didn't like the figurework on your last job. That's ambiguous. Do you mean you didn't like the figurework on your last job because it was too boring? because it was the same dreary adding of columns all day? Or do you mean that it was too diverse? that you never got a chance to learn to do your job as well as you wanted to because the procedure changed so often?

Unless you know the kind of figurework involved in the job for which you're interviewing, how do you know which remark is most helpful to the interviewer? Simply saying that you didn't like the figurework on your last job might cause the interviewer to eliminate you from consideration when the job actually involves exactly the kind of figurework you like.

That's why it's essential for you to hear about the job before you talk about yourself. It's difficult advice because we all like to talk about ourselves. But restrain yourself by relying on the wisdom of Proverb 18:13: "He who answers a matter before he hears it, / It is folly and shame to him."

> ● Rule 18 is to never talk about yourself
> until the right time in the interview. And that
> time is after you've found out about the job.
> Put the job before yourself in this case.

Another very popular question among interviewers is, "Where do you want to be in five years?" A more nebulous way of asking what is basically the same question is, "What are you looking for in a job?" Please understand that the interviewer has two concerns about you. First, he needs to be reassured that you can and will do the job well. You reassure him by letting your can-do attitude show during the interview.

His second concern is feeling confident you'll stay on the job for a reasonable length of time. All employees have a period of low productivity while getting started on a new job. The cost of that low productivity is best covered by spreading that period over the employee's tenure with the company. It's like a mortgage on a house; most of the payment is interest early on, and you don't work off much principal until some time has gone by.

One popular answer to the "Where do you want to be in five years?" type of question is, "I want *your* job" or "I intend to be the president of this company." Such an answer shows more than confidence: it shows aggression and arrogance. Nothing could be more distinct from the positive attitude that employers hire so eagerly.

Rather, you'll want to answer the question humbly, which is to say honestly. Certainly your progress through the organization is dependent on many, many factors, and you should acknowledge your understanding of that fact of life. All you can really say with honesty is that you're committed to being the best at the job you've been asked to do, now and in the future.

Which of the two answers would you rather hear: the pushy, offensive one or the forthright one? There's no place for arrogance in a good interview.

But there's no place for silence, either. A polite, enthusiastic response is necessary to every question the interviewer asks, including the one about your salary requirements. Some applicants show a reluctance to discuss this vital issue with the interviewer. They appear to be almost embarrassed at expecting to be paid for their labors. Why this should be, I've never understood.

The Lord related in Matthew 20:1–16 the story of the man who hired workers for his vineyard. The theme of the entire story revolves around the workers' wages. Some of the workers were rather surprised by the salary structure in that vineyard. The time to clarify salary-related issues is before you start a job, not after, as those vineyard workers learned to their dismay. There should be no discomfort associated with a discussion of salary.

Of course, it may be that the job is more important than the pay, at least at first. That's often the case with a candidate who's in a position to be flexible in salary in order to get a start at a new and desirable job. When the interviewer asks about your salary requirements, he clearly wants to know whether the company can afford you. Let him know.

The interviewer also wants to know how long the company can expect to keep you. Again, always remember the interviewer's concerns about turnover. He wants to keep you forever; he doesn't want to go through the advertising, screening, and interviewing processes all over again for the job you're going to fill. He wants to be sure that you're satisfied with what the company can afford to pay and that you'll continue to be satisfied with that job and that pay.

Accordingly, the interviewer's questions sometimes appear to be challenging; his remarks might make it seem that he doesn't share your enthusiasm for the job. He might ask questions along the lines of, "Why do you want to work here?" or "Why do you want this job?" When answering, use enough enthusiasm for both of you.

Because the interviewer finds that promotion creates more work for him, there's also a sense in which he considers every job to be a dead-end job. It influences his "Where do you want to be in five years?" question, too; he thinks you'll be in the same job you're discussing today.

But you know something the interviewer may not often think about: you know there's no such thing as a dead-end job. You know the Lord opens doors you didn't even know existed. You know the secret to being promoted is the same as the secret to getting hired in the first place: your positive, enthusiastic attitude.

Consequently, the interviewer's requests of the "Tell me why you want this job" variety give you the opportunity to really let your eagerness and enthusiasm shine all over the place.

Recognizing that there's no such thing as a dead-end job helps with your salary discussion, too. It might lead you to consider tempering your salary requirements to land a job with a promising future, provided your family responsibilities permit that. It also serves as a reminder that arrogant demands about the chances for promotion before you've even gotten the job can be detrimental to your success. Honesty and an earnest desire to help the interview along work well in responding to a question such as "What are your salary requirements?" You can truthfully say, "I'm ready to be flexible for a good opportunity. What is the salary range for the job?"

Notice that the exchange of remarks in the preceding paragraph follows a pattern: acknowledging the interviewer's question with a polite and truthful response, followed by your request for specific information. This pattern is useful for keeping the interview on a smooth course. It's helpful for both of you and can be used for just about every question the interviewer asks, at least in the early stages of your interview. When you know enough about the position, you can make definite, precise statements.

ATTITUDE WORDS

When you answer questions in an interview, use what I call "attitude words." Attitude words are powerful words. They're the words that employers like to hear applicants use when describing themselves. They're also the words that come naturally from the mouths of people who remember daily the many blessings God has given them.

Internalizing attitude words, making them a part of you, using them unconsciously in everyday conversation, will help ensure that both you and the interviewer share that friendly feeling when an interview is over. The more you both feel that way, the better are the chances that the interviewer will offer a job.

Attitude words have a positive feeling about them. They display confidence in the speaker and instill confidence in the listener. They're the kind of words you like to hear from your doctor or from the pilot of an airliner on which you're flying. They're the kind of words that people think of when they describe someone by that overused adjective *professional*. They're the kind of words that will make people feel about you the way you want them to feel: cordial, admiring, and respectful. They're the kind of words that help to change you for the better by changing the way you see life; as the writer Joseph Chilton Pearce has put it, "A change in world view can change the world viewed."

But there's a far more practical reason for you to develop an affirmative vocabulary. After thousands and thousands of interviews, I'm convinced that you have only about two minutes in which to make a favorable impression. And there's plenty of research that will support that personal observation. Two minutes is all it takes to identify about 80 percent of those candidates who will be invited to go on to the next stage of interviewing. It's really not very much time, is it?

Do you see why I want you to use powerful, affirmative attitude words early on in our conversation? Do you see that using those words is one of the very few ways you can *quickly demonstrate* your positive attitude?

I can't give you a list of all the attitude words; the supply is endless. What I will do, though, is give you a list of just a few of the attitude words that *I like to hear* during an interview. And here's another insider tip: all the other personnel people like to hear them, too. Then I'll suggest an exercise that will help you make these words a part of you.

Here are a few of my favorites:

ability, capability
accomplish, achieve, accomplishment, achievement
accurate, precise, accuracy, precision
active, action
attitude
cheerful
commitment, determination, determined
confident, confidence
contribute, contribution, share
discipline, disciplined
dynamic
eager
efficient, efficiency, effective
energy, energetic, hard-working
enthusiastic
excel
flexible, adaptable
goals, objectives
happy
participate, cooperate, recommend, help
perform, performance, produce
positive
ready
reliable, dependable, steady, consistent
responsible, responsibility
results
sincere, sincerity
strong, strengthen

success
thorough, careful, deliberate
timeliness
willing, willingness

The use of these words is like your attitude itself: it must be a part of you, and it can't be faked. Most of the how-to-find-a-job books contain similar lists. One calls them the "Action Words." Another calls its list the "Professional Vocabulary" or "ProVo." I can always spot an applicant who read one of those books recently by his stilted, formal, and clumsy use of the words in the list.

Using such words truthfully and honestly requires you to *own* the words. The way to acquire them for keeps is through an exercise. Of course. What else did you expect? Every day, beginning today, write one of the words on an index card or a piece of paper. Then write a short sentence on the same piece of paper using that word to describe yourself. Put the paper in your wallet.

Later on in the day, when you're on the train or waiting in a reception room or otherwise unoccupied, take out the paper and write another sentence. Let your target be the generation of five short sentences before you finally go to bed at night. In other words, don't just photocopy the list and promise that you'll memorize it later. Learn to use the words and to use them naturally.

Let me give you an example to get you started. The word *eager* occurs about a third of the way down the list. Many people use the word *anxious* when they should use *eager,* as in "I'm anxious to get a job." But the words don't mean the same thing at all.

Eager implies a keen and avid interest in a task; it shows the pleasure with which you anticipate starting a task. But *anxious*—like *anxiety,* the word on which it's based—has to do with worry and fear. These negative words have to be squeezed out of your vocabulary by attitude words. Write sentences such as "I'm eager to take on the challenge of a new job" or "I'm what they call an 'eager beaver'" that can also be used to respond to a question about your strengths and weaknesses. Here's another example: "I eagerly anticipate an affirmative response to my interview," which you can use in a thank-you note if you'd like.

If you think of attitude words in addition to the ones listed above (there's no limit to them, and I think you get the idea of their characteristics), go right ahead and do the exercise with those words. You'll have a job long, long before you exhaust the list of possible attitude words, but why stop? Learn to use positive words in daily conversation and you'll find it improves your whole outlook on life.

● **Rule 19 is that if positive attitude words are the only ones in your vocabulary, you'll find yourself voicing negative thoughts less often. As a result, your attitude will be more affirmative, enthusiastic, sincere, and joyous.**

CHAPTER 15

Job Hunting While Already Employed

= ◊ =

Not only can the words we use to talk about life be powerful, but the circumstances of life in which we find ourselves can often be powerful as well. Consider, for example, how excellent is your situation if you're able to look for a new job at the same time you enjoy the blessing of already being employed. One obviously powerful aspect of this situation is that you're under far less economic pressure than has been the case with so many other examples in this book. And that's real power!

But being able to look for a new job while currently being employed yields another blessing that may not be readily apparent. To understand it, let me urge you once again to get in the habit of doing what I've recommended before: adopt the prospective employer's point of view, and determine the kind of person you would want to hire if you were in his place. You'll find that he wants to hire someone of sound moral principles, just as you would. Integrity is always important to employers, but it's especially so today.

THE VALUE OF INTEGRITY

Many people today ignore traditional Judeo-Christian virtues in their quest for professional achievement or commercial success. Indeed, we see examples of greed and dishonesty everywhere. For example, an important continuing news story in Chicago at the time of this writing involves allegations of corruption among local judges. You don't have to live in Chicago; we can all remember similar stories in our own localities. Such charges sometimes make it seem that even our most trusted officials may be unable to cope with the vicious temptations put in the path of the ambitious.

In this kind of environment, is it surprising to you that employers will put a premium on employees who can be trusted? Honesty has always been the best policy; now it is the most productive policy for people who want a job. In fact, it's the first characteristic I look for when hiring an employee for my own business.

Of course, you have a head start when it comes to integrity. I'm sure you try to be honest, truthful, and fair in all your dealings. You try to behave in such a way as not to have to be ashamed of yourself. But how do you let a prospective employer, a total stranger, know that you esteem highly your own integrity and that you will bring that integrity to the job?

That's where being employed while looking for another job turns to your natural advantage. At some point, you'll be called by an interviewer and will be asked when it's convenient for you to come for an interview. I have read job-hunting books that advise you to *always* say "whenever you'd like" or "my time is your time." On the surface, such remarks might impress you as cooperative and helpful. You might feel they mark you as a "team player."

But if you adopt the interviewer's point of view, what would you think when you heard this remark? You'd probably think the same thing I do; you'd wonder how the applicant will justify absence from his job to his current employer who's paying him to be there. When an employed applicant (notice that an *unemployed* applicant is quite another matter) tells me he can see me immediately or at my pleasure, that applicant starts with one strike against him. I consider that he's cheating his present employer. I have no reason to think he'd treat my client any differently if I advised my client to hire him.

The moral position of a job seeker who's employed while looking for a new job is to choose one of two courses of action: (1) take time off with permission (which usually means taking a vacation day or arranging to put in "make-up time," which might mean your present employer will know that you're looking for another job), or (2) arrange interviews on one's own time (which may mean skipping lunch or arranging your interview in the evening or early morning or on the weekend). In either event, you can still show how cooperative you are by offering the interviewer a choice of times at his convenience within your legitimate time boundaries.

Of course, it is always appropriate that you inform the interviewer of the circumstances. That is, let him know that you choose *as a matter of conscience* not to "bootleg" time from your job. If you agree to the lunch hour, let him know that you're skipping lunch and using your own time rather than your employer's. But never steal time from your employer, and never let an interviewer develop the erroneous impression that you are.

It's remarkable how many how-to books are insensitive to this basic issue of ethics. It's also equally remarkable how powerful an attraction the interviewer will feel for you as a result of letting him know immediately where you stand morally. It's a totally honest display of your proper attitude. It makes for you that good first impression that everyone knows is so important. And best of all, it comes about as a natural and logical consequence of putting your Christian beliefs into practice.

Some people might object that following the practice of interviewing only on your own time might disqualify you for some interviews, that the interviewer might take offense if you're not instantly available. I can assure you that this is not the case. We personnel people are a lot like real estate sales people: we're accustomed to working nights and weekends to earn our commissions. Those of us who can't synchronize our schedules to the needs of our clients and applicants tend to seek other careers after a very short period of time.

THE NEED FOR PRUDENCE

It should go without saying that it's common sense to be prudent in your remarks to your coworkers and your supervisor when looking for another job. I have found a few companies that are tolerant of an employee who feels a need to examine new opportunities, but only a few. Usually, such forbearance and understanding are not the case. So, the rule is this: there's no compulsion to inform your present employer that you're looking for another job if you don't let that search affect what he's paying you to do.

Looking for a new job while still working is not at all uncommon, as we all know. But concern that one's employer will learn of a job search and fear of the unpleasant confrontation that could follow make some job seekers afraid to respond to the so-called blind-box ad. Blind-box ads don't identify the employer, and they instruct the applicant only to write to "Box Number so-and-so." The fear, of course, is that your current employer is the one who placed the ad. Blind-box ads, however, have become for a variety of reasons the standard type of ad in many industries and localities. Fear of responding to blind-box ads will eliminate a very rich source of potential jobs.

Therefore, don't let the fear that your resume might be sent to your present employer stop you from responding to blind-box ads. All major newspapers have ways of protecting you from such a serious miscommunication. For your reference, here is the policy of the *Chicago Tribune,* the newspaper with which I am most familiar. Be advised that the *Tribune's* policy is typical but not necessarily universal. So before you respond to such ads, call the classified advertising department of the paper in which you saw the ad and ask about its procedure.

To respond safely to a blind-box ad in the *Chicago Tribune,* put your resume inside an envelope addressed as indicated in the ad. Then put *that* envelope in a second, somewhat larger envelope addressed to the newspaper's classified ad department. Write "Do Not Forward to (name of your present company)" on the *outer* envelope, and that instruction will be followed. You're protected. Should it happen that it was indeed your employer who placed the ad, your resume will be destroyed. So if you don't receive a response from a blind-box ad, don't feel too bad. But go ahead and send your resume; trust the newspaper to recognize and fulfill its responsibility to you.

RESPONSIBILITY TO YOUR PRESENT EMPLOYER

As a currently employed job seeker, you must recognize a responsibility of your own, one that an unemployed job seeker doesn't share: a responsibility to your present employer. When you receive your new job offer, your perspective must shift immediately from job seeking to leave taking. Give appropriate notice: two weeks on most jobs, but longer if the responsibility level of the job you're leaving is great. Offer to train a replacement. If you're involved in the kind of activities that take place over time as opposed to those that start and finish on a day-to-day basis, write a summary of the status of those activities.

In other words, be as cooperative and helpful as you can be once you give notice. This corresponds to the advice to never burn your bridges behind you, and it ensures you a reference that's as glowing as your attitude toward your new job. More than that, it's reflective of the respect that you and your employer owe each other.

But don't prepare for your departure just yet; there's one crucial step in the interviewing process that you have to learn before you get that big job offer. It's a step that helps avoid a common mistake made by the currently employed job seeker—and by the unemployed job seeker—the first-time job seeker—the young—the not-so-young—my relatives—just about everybody, in fact.

This mistake accounts more than any other single factor for an interviewer's failure to appreciate your enthusiasm, confidence, determination, sincerity, and cheerfulness. And you must learn from the next chapter how to avoid it.

CHAPTER 16

How to Get the Offer

= ◇ =

There's a mistake that applicants frequently commit at the end of the interview. It's a mistake so elementary, so easy to avoid, and yet so common that you might find it difficult to believe. But this basic error is committed every day by people who otherwise interview well. Let's see where we are now, and then we'll see how costly this little mistake can be.

Look what you've accomplished so far if you've taken a precise, workmanlike approach to job hunting. You've become aware of the vital importance of your joyous, confident attitude, and you've taken steps to recover it. You've become aware of the fallacies, myths, and distractions that stand in the way of the unwary, and you've demolished them. You've become aware of your worth, and you've been comforted by the fact that the Lord shares your assessment of yourself. You've come to understand that no obstacle stands in your path unless you permit it to do so and that, even though that obstacle is a mountain, there's no mountain too high to be crossed with the Lord's help. You have, in the words of Ephesians 6:11, "put on the whole armor of God, that you may be able to stand against the wiles of the devil."

You've learned the truth about the mechanics of job hunting. You've learned how simple and inexpensive it can be, in spite of all the printed and spoken words that encourage you to gold-plate your efforts. You've learned the value of being "firstest with the mostest." You've seen that the way you dress, act, and speak during an interview must correspond to your Christian image of yourself. That image is a result of faith, self-respect, good manners, and old-fashioned common sense, all of which you possess in abundance. You've even begun to develop a natural and comfortable use of language that will display your attitude automatically in everyday life.

You've developed to the point that you're irresistible to employers. You know how to find out where the jobs are, and you know how to get them. And eventually, maybe even immediately, you'll score in the job market. Big. Because you *know* what a winner the Lord has made of you.

Now suppose you've come to the end of an interview that's been the best one you've ever had. You feel good about having participated in it, and you know the interviewer feels the same way.

But wait. There's one thing left to do before you leave. Everything you've done to this point has shown and proved your positive attitude. That's essential to a productive interview. But it's not the reason you're there. You're there to get a job, and you haven't yet got it.

It is truly astounding how many otherwise successful candidates forget to do the simple thing that must close every productive interview. If you want the job, you must let the interviewer know. You must show your interest in the job he has to offer.

You must ask for the job.

Be forthright. Be assertive. Say, "I want to work for your company." Say, "I'm excited by this opportunity; I'd like to have this job." Say whatever you're comfortable saying that shows you want to work and work *there* at *that* job.

Be candid at this point. Don't hold back. If you're a little short of the qualifications the job needs, determine to make up the deficiency as soon as possible, and tell the interviewer of that determination. Let him know that you'll acquire any skills you lack. Above all, be sure you let him know what you *will* bring to the job.

Never neglect to ask for the job, and do it with the most shining attitude you can muster. Then continue helping the interviewer, as you have done to this point, by asking him what happens next. Ask whether he needs for you to meet with anyone else in the organization. Make his task easier by letting him know of at least two alternative times when you'd be happy to take the next step. If you're so enthused about the job that the next step could be *right now* as far as you're concerned, tell him so.

And when you leave, tell him that you enjoyed the interview. Let him know that it was a pleasure meeting him and that you look forward to seeing him again. In other words, leave him with your "friendly four" elements of greeting: a firm handshake, a glowing smile, direct eye contact, and use of his name. They give just as much pleasure to both of you at departure time as they do at arrival time.

But what if the employer doesn't want you?

I confess that I played a trick on you with that last line. I phrased it to help you test your attitude. There's something called "rejection" that bothers some people. But not you. The fact is, there's *no way* the employer could not want you if you've properly displayed your enthusiastic attitude and it's genuine. What can happen is that the employer may want somebody else *more*. And that's entirely different, isn't it?

You're not the only person in the world with a good attitude. And thank God for that! The only applicants you'll lose out to are others who have the same outstanding attitude. But there sadly aren't that many of us, are there?

When a company chooses another candidate over you, the successful candidate should consider himself a winner. But that doesn't make you a loser! Vince Lombardi claimed that the Green Bay Packers never "lost" a single football game in his history as head coach; but sometimes time ran out while the other team had more points on the board.

Sometimes another candidate "wins" the job. But you're a winner, too; the Lord won't let it be otherwise. If the candidate chosen hadn't come along, you would have been offered the job. So, you'll get the next one.

You'll probably need more than one successful, pleasurable interview before you find the right job. But that won't discourage you; you're prepared for more than one attempt before your inevitable success. Thomas Edison is said to have had the same experience. He was trying to invent the light bulb, and he'd been working on it for many years without success. One day a reporter asked him how many experiments he'd done so far. "Nine thousand," Edison said. Then he smiled.

The reporter couldn't understand how the great man could smile cheerfully after all that fruitless work. "There are only so many elements and compounds," Edison told the reporter. "I figure it might take as many as ten thousand experiments before I find the right combination of them. And that's why I'm smiling. Only a thousand more to go!"

● **Rule 20 is that each interview will make you a better applicant, better equipped to take up the job the Lord has set aside for you, more prepared to recognize that job when He**

reveals it to you. And it won't take you ten thousand interviews to find it, either. The Lord wouldn't do that to you.

Somewhere out there is a job with your name on it. Go and get it!